Heaven is Like Eternal Sex

And Other Things You Really Desire

18 Daily Readings

Jim Sandman

Carolyn,
I'm praying
this book uplifts your
spirit !
Jim Sandman
Eph 1:3

Cover Design By:
Tony Rollo - Nashville - **www.TonyRollo.com**

Photo/image credits:
Front cover – Shutterstock, Inc.
Back cover – scenic photo by the author

Published via Kindle Direct Publishing

Heaven is...

Reader Comments

"After reading the entirety of your new book, I personally believe you will have great success. With the subject matter you are exploring and your vision into this subject - you are truly onto something important that will be more than appreciated by any reader."
 - Tony Rollo - Nashville Producer / Feature Filmmaker / Honor Society / Actor / www.TonyRollo.com

"Sandman's text does a good job explaining how basic human desires can best be managed by applying Christ's teachings to them in our daily lives."
 - William Ford, past President Federal Reserve Bank of Atlanta, retired Professor of Economics and Finance, Middle Tennessee State University, US Navy Submarine veteran

"Jim Sandman's creativity takes us way beyond the eye-catching title of this book. As I read through these pages, I was drawn deeper into a beautiful and encouraging vision of what is real and lasting; to the kind of hope we all desperately need in this world of confusing and disappointing counterfeits."
 - Peter Schmidt, Professional Counselor, author of *How Did Love Become A Reality Show?*

CONTENTS

Heaven is…

Introduction

You may be asking, quite understandably:

- How can this guy claim that Heaven is like eternal sex? Has he been there and back?
- Why does he compare God's holy dwelling to having sex?
- Does Heaven even exist?

Read on.

Any book that talks about Heaven, in my humble opinion, should have at least two sources to back it up:

1) statements from the first book that describes Heaven - the Bible - still the world's #1 bestselling book ever, and
2) eyewitness accounts, from folks who have had a glimpse of Heaven through a near-death experience (NDE).

I will share both for your thoughtful consideration. Then you can decide if I'm deluded... or not. And if you're skeptical about the Bible, I get that. There was a time in my life I paid no attention to it. But I soon realized that its Author was paying attention to me. I only ask that you read the verses I share with an open mind.

Not everyone has the same level of longing for the various desires I discuss in this book. Some folks have a deep need to feel loved; others may care less (at least outwardly).

Some may not like music, others thrive on it. Some may not like sex for various reasons; others ponder it every day (or hour!).

But all of us, I would venture to say, can relate to at least a few of these deep-seated desires.

The good news is: Our Creator wants to fulfill those desires in our life…completely. King David wrote,

"Take delight in the LORD, and He will give you your heart's desires" (Psalm 37:4).

The bad news: we're selfish, proud and stubborn. We'd rather try to fulfil them in our own way, and with our own time schedule.

But how would you like to have *every* desire completely satisfied, and for *eternity*?

In the first century A.D., in his letter to the believers at Ephesus (on the west coast of modern-day Turkey), Apostle Paul wrote,

"Praise the God and Father of our Lord Jesus Christ, who has blessed us in Christ with every spiritual blessing in the heavens" (Ephesians 1:3).

Therefore, some blessings and benefits of Heaven are already available to those "in Christ" (Christians), albeit in imperfect vessels on this earth, for now.

But, just imagine how much more satisfying they will be in Heaven! And though these blessings of Heaven are promised to Christians, they are also longed for by those who do not claim to be (or even want to be) a Christian.

Just ask anyone: What do you long for most? I'll bet it's closely related to one of the desires I discuss herein.

Have you noticed that we humans all crave for something, and when we think we've found it, we find ourselves craving and searching more? I believe that the elusive "more" will be found ultimately in Heaven. And people who have had NDE's attest that Heaven is the most beautiful and satisfying place they have ever experienced. They didn't want to come back to life on Earth, but they did. Their time was not up yet. They have a message they want to tell the rest of us.[1]

Simply put, the things that you and I really want, deep down, are what our Creator has already promised us. Solomon, the wise and wealthy King of Israel from 970 – 931 B.C., wrote,

"He has also put eternity in their hearts..." (Ecclesiastes 3:11).

You and I have a part of us that is eternal; we will dwell forever...somewhere. This "eternity" within us makes us hungry and thirsty for the eternal. And only Eternity will fill it.

C. S. Lewis wrote, "If we find ourselves with a desire that nothing in this world can satisfy, the most probable explanation is that we were made for another world." [2]

Yes, we were made for another world – Heaven, and the coming New Earth.

The prophet Isaiah, who lived in the eighth century B.C., wrote God's promise:

"For I will create a new heaven and a new earth; the past events will not be remembered or come to mind" (Isaiah 65:17).

I wrote this book to encourage the reader to seriously consider what your loving Creator has to offer you, and come to the realization that what you truly long for, He provides, through faith and trust in His only Son, Jesus Christ, who died in our place to win us back to God. We only need to admit our sin (selfish pride, stubbornness) and accept His free gift of forgiveness and eternal life by faith in Christ (John 3:16).

However, if a person rejects God's gift of forgiveness and eternal life, that person will see NONE of these desires fulfilled, *neither in this life nor in the next.*

In fact, that person will stand condemned and be eternally tormented. Contrary to popular opinion, Hell is *not* a big party. Read Luke 16:19-31.

Also, consider what Jesus said:

"For God loved the world in this way: He gave His One and Only Son, so that everyone who believes in Him will not perish but have eternal life. For God did not send His Son into the world that He might condemn the world, but that the world might be saved through Him. Anyone who believes in Him is not condemned, but anyone who does not believe is already condemned, because he has not believed in the name of the One and Only Son of God.

"This, then, is the judgment: The light has come into the world, and people loved darkness rather than the light because their deeds were evil. For everyone who practices wicked things hates the light and avoids it, so that his deeds may not be exposed. But anyone who lives by the truth comes to the light, so that his works may be shown to be accomplished by God" (John 3:16-21).

For those who are already "in Christ", I pray the truths in these pages will strengthen your faith, and help you share the blessings of Heaven to those around you.

Heaven, not hell, is where the real party will be!

At the end of each brief chapter are two questions. To gain the most from this book, please take time to ponder an answer. Most are simple Yes or No questions, but you may want to expand your answer with more detail. Maybe write them down in a diary or journal, or include them in a review of this book on Amazon, or post them on social media. Your story will likely help someone else.

"You reveal the path of life to me;
in Your presence is abundant joy;
in Your right hand are eternal pleasures."

King David
Psalm 16:11

Heaven is...

1

Like Eternal Sex

I could have placed this chapter at the very end of the book, as a climax of sorts. But I reckoned that folks would flip to the back of the book first, so I'll save you the trouble.

You're welcome.

I'm a huge fan of Mark Twain (Samuel Clemens) and his writings, and not only because he's my second cousin (five times removed – which, with a dollar might get me a candy bar), but also because of his humorous wit, and his way with words.

In his *"Letters from the Earth,"* speaking from the perspective of Satan who criticizes mankind, he says: "He has imagined a heaven, and has left entirely out of it the supremest of all his delights...sexual intercourse!"[1]

Firstly, whether or not Mr. Twain believed that Satan or Heaven were real, I'm not sure. But if he didn't, I would respond by saying Heaven was not "imagined" by man.

According to the Bible, it existed *before* man was created. Indeed, Satan himself was cast out of Heaven when he tried to exalt himself above God (Ezekiel 28:17).

So, Satan knows all too well that there's a Heaven. (See also Ezekiel 28: 11-17; Isaiah 14:14-15; Luke 10:18, Revelation 20:10)

If Mr. Twain *did* believe in a real Heaven, then his word "imagine" simply refers to one's attempt to picture what Heaven is like.

Secondly, I would agree with Mr. Twain that sexual intercourse is the "supremest of all his [mankind's] delights." God designed it that way when He made us male and female, to become one flesh.

"So God created man in His own image; He created him in the image of God; He created them male and female" (Genesis 1:27).
"This is why a man leaves his father and mother and bonds with his wife, and they become one flesh" (Genesis 2:24).

Thirdly, I would concur with Mr. Twain that there is no sexual intercourse in Heaven. This is not because God doesn't want any lovemaking in Heaven, but because there is no need for reproduction, a command given to Adam and Eve to "be fruitful and multiply and fill the earth" (Genesis 1:28).

And there have been people who had near-death experiences (clinically dead for a brief period, then revived) who describe residents of the present Heaven as having no genitals.[2]

However, in the *new* Heaven and *new* Earth, the Bible teaches we'll have resurrected bodies. Will our bodies be distinctly male and female? I believe they will, as a carryover from our earthly lives.

But the purpose of sex (reproduction in the old Earth) will be fulfilled, and therefore not necessary.

Randy Alcorn, in his excellent book *Heaven* writes "...there may...be some way in which the intimacy and pleasure we now know as sex will also be fulfilled in some higher form... I do know that sex was designed by God, and I don't expect him to discard it without replacing it with something better."[3]

So if there's no sex in Heaven, how can I claim that Heaven will be like eternal sex?

The Bible teaches that in Heaven, there will be a consummation of the marriage between its King of kings - Jesus Christ - and His bride, the Church (born again Christians – see John 3). And we all know what a bride and groom enjoy when they "consummate" their marriage. Our union with Christ in Heaven will be an everlasting union, overflowing with eternal love and intimacy.

To be blunt – I believe it will be like a sexual orgasm...that lasts *forever*!

I do not mean to suggest that there's eternal sex in Heaven, but that there's eternal intimacy and ecstasy in Heaven – and it will *immensely* surpass the delight we experience on Earth during physical sex.[4]

Consider this...

The whole concept of marriage between a man and a woman, instituted by God in the book of Genesis, is a beautiful picture of the relationship between Christ and His bride.

Even in the debate between evolution and creationism, the topic of sex should be included. Thomas Purifoy, Jr., producer, writer, and director of *Is Genesis History?* writes, "Sex is one of the essential parts of God's creation, something only He could create in order to show forth His glory. If He dedicated an entire book of the Bible to it (The Song of Songs), it's something we should strive to understand from a Biblical perspective. After all, God put a deep fascination within us toward sex because He wants us to get a sense of the complex relationship He has with us. It's no coincidence that the Bible begins with a marriage and ends with a marriage."[5]

In Genesis (first book in the Bible) we have the first marriage – Adam and Eve. In Revelation (last book in the Bible) we learn of the marriage between Jesus Christ and His bride - all believers.

The prophet Isaiah wrote,

"Indeed, your husband is your Maker—His name is Yahweh of Hosts—and the Holy One of Israel is your Redeemer; He is called the God of all the earth" (Isaiah 54:5).

Paul the apostle wrote,

"Husbands, love your wives, just as Christ loved the church and gave Himself for her to make her holy, cleansing her with the washing of water by the word. He did this to present the church to Himself in splendor, without spot or wrinkle or anything like that, but holy and blameless." (See Ephesians 5:22-33)

John, the longest living of the twelve disciples of Christ wrote about the vision of Heaven God gave him. In the vision, John heard many voices saying,

"Let us be glad, rejoice, and give Him glory, because the marriage of the Lamb has come, and His wife has prepared herself. She was given fine linen to wear, bright and pure. For the fine linen represents the righteous acts of the saints." John goes on to write what the angel accompanying him said, "Then he said to me, 'Write: Those invited to the marriage feast of the Lamb are fortunate!' He also said to me, 'These words of God are true'" (Revelation 19:7-9).

Many Bible teachers have explained the parallels between human marriage (a Jewish wedding, in particular) and Christ's marriage to the Church.[6] These parallels are no coincidence. They have eternal significance for believers in Christ.

Solomon, King David's son, who succeeded him on the throne of Israel, said:

"Let your fountain be blessed, and take pleasure in the wife of your youth. A loving doe, a graceful fawn—let her breasts always satisfy you; be lost in her love forever" (Proverbs 5:18-19).

Men, can you imagine the pleasure of being "lost in her love forever"?

The Song of Solomon (also called The Song of Songs) in the Old Testament is a beautiful, poetic romance story of the love and intimacy shared between King Solomon and the Shulamite woman he courted and married. It gets pretty graphic, so kids may giggle at the wording, but it illustrates wonderfully the intimacy that Jesus Christ offers His bride.

Solomon wrote:

"How beautiful you are, my darling. How very beautiful! Behind your veil, your eyes are doves. Your hair is like a flock of goats streaming down Mount Gilead" (Song of Solomon 4:1).

She says, "His mouth is sweetness. He is absolutely desirable. This is my love, and this is my friend, young women of Jerusalem" (Song of Solomon 5:16).

Put simply, sex between a husband and a wife is a gift from God, and it's a model of the *eternal intimacy* between Christ and His Church.

I don't know about you, but I can't wait! The excited anticipation of love and oneness on our wedding night here on Earth is but a tiny sample of what believers will experience in Heaven and on the New Earth with God.

God says, "I will take you to be My wife forever. I will take you to be My wife in righteousness, justice, love, and compassion. I will take you to be My wife in faithfulness, and you will *know* Yahweh" (Hosea 2:19-20).

That word "know" is significant. In the Bible, it is often used to express a close, intimate relationship, as in the above verse. But other variations of the same word mean sexual intercourse.

"And Adam knew his wife; and she conceived..." (Genesis 4:1, KJV. See also 1 Samuel 1:19; 1 Kings 1:4). The Hebrew word here is יָדַע, or yada (pronounced yaw-dah'), meaning "to know carnally."

So, in Heaven believers will experience the most intimate relationship with our Creator, full of ecstasy...forever!

One NDEr named Khalida was so overtaken with awe at the beauty of God that he could only fall to his knees and bask in His glorious light.[7]

Another said of Heaven:

- "It's the pinnacle of everything there is. Of energy, of love especially, of warmth, of beauty." - anonymous Dutch NDEr.[8]

For more eye-witness stories, see Bodie Thoene and Samaa Habib's book, *Face to Face with Jesus: A Former Muslim's Extraordinary Journey to Heaven and Encounter with the God of Love* (Bloomington, MN: Chosen, a division of Baker Publishing Group, 2014).

In his book *Miracles*, C. S. Lewis had something to say about sexuality, too:

"The letter and spirit of Scripture, and of all Christianity, forbid us to suppose that life in the New Creation will be a sexual life; and this reduces our imagination to the withering alternatives either of bodies which are hardly recognizable as human bodies at all or else of a perpetual fast.

"As regards the fast, I think our present outlook might be like that of a small boy who, on being told that the sexual act was the highest bodily pleasure, should immediately ask whether you ate chocolates at the same time. On receiving the answer 'No,' he might regard [the] absence of chocolates as the chief characteristic of sexuality.

"In vain would you tell him that the reason why lovers in their raptures don't bother about chocolates is that they have something better to think of. The boy knows chocolate: he does not know the positive thing that excludes it. We are in the same position. We know the sexual life; we do not know, except in glimpses, the other thing which, in Heaven, will leave no room for it."[9]

He who created sex as a way of expressing love physically between a man and a woman AND for the purpose of reproduction has also prepared an even better gift of intimacy and ecstasy in Heaven that will last an eternity, for all those who are part of His bride, the Church.

Would *you* like to experience an eternal spiritual orgasm after your body dies?

Have you accepted Jesus' marriage proposal?

"When a man is in union with his wife in a spirit of holiness and purity, the Divine Presence is with them."

Nachmanides (A.D. 1194 – 1270)

2

True Love and Friendship

Have you ever felt lonely?

Do you long for someone to love you, even if they know your weaknesses and failures?

Have you experienced the joy of being truly loved?

Would you want to live forever in love, and in the presence of the One who made you, died for you, and prays for you?

Love.

It's our deepest need. Stronger than hate. It's the finest thing around. Myriads of songs throughout history have touted it. Everyone wants and needs true love.

What song about love can you think of? Go ahead, sing a few bars...

God is all about Love. Why don't we learn it from Him?

When asked what the greatest commandment was, Jesus said:

"Love the Lord your God with all your heart, with all your soul, and with all your mind. This is the greatest and most important command. The second is like it: Love your neighbor as yourself. All the Law and the Prophets depend on these two commands" (Matthew 22:36-40).

Just think. All the "do's and don'ts" in the Bible can be summed up by:

1) loving God, and

2) loving people.

Wouldn't this world be a better place if we all (especially Christians) loved God and others as we should?

I grew up reading and enjoying Charles Schulz's *Peanuts* books and daily comic strip (still do). Like most of us, Linus struggles with loving people, especially his sister Lucy sometimes. From the Nov 12, 1959 strip[1]…

PEANUTS © 1959 Peanuts Worldwide LLC. Dist. By ANDREWS MCMEEL SYNDICATION. Reprinted with permission. All rights reserved.

Truth.

Some folks are difficult to love, others quite easy. And we ourselves are sometimes hard to love. Just ask your spouse or someone else who is close to you.

Here's another truth:

God not only tells us to love, He *IS* love.

Where did "love" come from, anyway?

The apostle John wrote:

"Dear friends, let us love one another, because *love is from God,* and everyone who loves has been born of God and knows God. The one who does not love does not know God, because God is love" (1 John 4:8, emphasis mine).

Where God is, love dwells. Love never fails. (See 1 Corinthians 13)

The apostle John was one of the three closest disciples of Jesus, and is known as the "beloved disciple." His writings in the New Testament are full of references to love – loving God and loving others.

"And we have seen and we testify that the Father has sent His Son as the world's Savior. Whoever confesses that Jesus is the Son of God — God remains in him and he in God.

"And we have come to know and to believe the love that God has for us. God is love, and the one who remains in love remains in God, and God remains in him" (1 John 4: 14-16).

Also, Apostle Paul (formerly named Saul), in his letter to the church in Rome, said:

"For I am persuaded that not even death or life, angels or rulers, things present or things to come, hostile powers, height or depth, or any other created thing will have the power to separate us from the love of God that is in Christ Jesus our Lord!" (Romans 8:38-39).

And this is from a guy who would chase down and imprison Christians! (See Acts 8:3; Galatians 1:21-24)

Only God's love can enable us to love like He loves.

Let's stop looking for love in all the wrong places. I'll bet you can think of a few wrong places.

Twenty-year-old Ian McCormack found the greatest Love while clinically dead, after being stung by a school of box jellyfish four times - one sting can be fatal. After his NDE, he describes meeting with God:

"I felt totally exposed and transparent before God. You can wear masks before other people but you can't wear a mask before God. I felt ashamed and undone...My first thought was that this light was going to cast me back into the pit, but to my amazement a wave of pure unconditional love flowed over me.
It was the last thing I expected. Instead of judgement I was being washed with pure love; pure, unadulterated, clean, uninhibited, undeserved, love.
"It began to fill me up from the inside out...I found myself beginning to weep uncontrollably as the love became stronger and stronger. It was so clean and pure, no strings attached...This love was healing my heart and I began to understand that there is incredible hope for humankind in this love."[2]

Heaven for the Christian will include a joyous reunion with friends we knew on Earth, unlike hell, which will NOT be a big party with all our rowdy friends (See Matthew 25:46).

Pastor Don Piper was pronounced dead after a head-on crash with an 18-wheeler. Before regaining consciousness, he found himself in Heaven, where a crowd of people rushed toward him. They were all friends who had passed away.[3]

Heaven is a place where you will be surrounded by love.

Would you like to be in the very presence of Love itself?

I didn't ask if you've ever felt greatly loved. I'm asking, would you like to experience a love so wonderful, so glorious, so *personal* that you feel like you're the only person in the world and *all* Love is focused on *you*? Forever?[4]

Jesus said:

"No one has greater love than this, that someone would lay down his life for his friends" (John 15:13).

And that's what He did for you and me. And if we follow and obey Him, He calls us His friends. Because of Jesus, I will live forever in Heaven...with my best Friend.

Have you accepted His love and friend request yet?

If you have, does your life show others that He's your best Friend?

" You are My friends
if you do what I command you."

Jesus Christ
John 15:14

His commands:
1. Love God
2. Love others as yourself

3

Real Joy

Which is better: happiness or joy?

Merriam-Webster dictionary defines "joy" as:
- the emotion evoked by well-being, success, or good fortune or by the prospect of possessing what one desires: delight

The same dictionary defines "happiness" as:

- a state of well-being and contentment: joy

- a pleasurable or satisfying experience

Sometimes the two words are used interchangeably, and other times they can describe varying degrees of the same emotion. The "prospect of possessing what one desires" describes an element of hope that comes with joy.

I've always thought of joy as happiness on steroids. Joy is a much greater, longer-lasting, inner sense of exuberance that outlasts happiness, which is temporary, and based on external circumstances. Inner joy can be experienced amid the down times and difficult days.

David, the shepherd, musician, soldier, King of Judah, knew where joy could be found. He said:

"You reveal the path of life to me; in Your presence is abundant joy; in Your right hand are eternal pleasures" (Psalm 16:11).

Heaven will be "abundant joy" because we will be closest to God's loving and awe-inspiring presence. While we can sense God's presence here on this earth, we have only a taste of the real joy we can have once we're in Heaven.

The prophet Isaiah said it this way:

"Therefore the redeemed of the LORD shall return, and come with singing unto Zion; and everlasting joy shall be upon their head: they shall obtain gladness and joy; and sorrow and mourning shall flee away" (Isaiah 51:11, KJV).

I don't know about you, but "everlasting joy" sounds pretty good to me! And then there's the added benefit of no more sorrow and mourning.

The writer of Hebrews said:

"…keeping our eyes on Jesus, the source and perfecter of our faith, who for the joy that lay before Him endured a cross and despised the shame and has sat down at the right hand of God's throne" (Hebrews 12:2).

Jesus saw this "joy that lay before Him", and was therefore able to "endure the cross." We can do the same here on earth – keep focused on the real joy ahead in Heaven, and we can endure anything.

David said:

"You have put more joy in my heart than they have when their grain and new wine abound" (Psalm 4:7).

This joy from God is more than any temporary physical pleasure we can find during our earthly lives, even with an abundance of provisions – food or wine, houses or land.

Someone has said that JOY can truly be found by loving:

Jesus
Others
Yourself

This goes right along with what Jesus said about the two greatest commandments I mentioned in the previous chapter (Matthew 22:36-40). It's that simple.

Here's a truth that believers in Jesus can bank on: as sojourners in this life, we have a profound reality facing us every day. Whenever our world provides hints of Heaven, we have joy; and when it doesn't, we have comfort of better things to come.

In what ways does this world remind you of the next, bringing joy? For me, it's:

- when I look at the stars on a clear night, or a beautiful sunset, a fertile valley, a colorful mountain range, or the new flowers and buds on the trees at springtime.

- when I hear the cry of a newborn baby, the laughter of children, the sweet harmonies of a choir, or a J. S. Bach pipe organ prelude.

- when I feel the sympathetic touch from a loved one while grieving, or affection from my wife, or when one of my grandchildren sees me, exclaiming "Pappy !!" and runs to me with a big smile and a hug.

In what ways does this world *not* remind you of the next, bringing solace that better things lay ahead? For me, it's:

- when I see the destruction of wildfires, hurricanes, tornados, or earthquakes.

- when someone is abused, exploited, robbed, or murdered because of hate, prejudice, lust, or greed.

- when power-hungry tyrants deprive the citizens of individual human rights.

It's tremendously comforting to know that there's another world full of joy waiting for the "Christian pilgrim."

Why did Jesus come to Earth and teach us about God? To give us joy – His joy.

In John 15:9-11 He said:

"As the Father has loved Me, I have also loved you. Remain in My love. If you keep My commands you will remain in My love, just as I have kept My Father's commands and remain in His love.

"I have spoken these things to you so that My joy may be in you and your joy may be complete."

The joy here on Earth that we can have by basking in God's love and obeying Him is one thing. But this is only a taste of the full joy found in Heaven. It will be exponentially better... and everlasting!

Captain Dale Black was a commercial airline pilot. But one day, when flying a Piper Navajo with two friends on board, they stalled and crashed. His two friends died, and Dale survived, but only after the most amazing near-death experience, that included an indescribable joy during his brief visit to Heaven. There was absolutely nothing bad there to diminish it. No "buzz killers." Rather, *everything* was magnificent and fabulous.[1]

C. S. Lewis also wrote, "Joy is the serious business of Heaven."[2]

If we want true joy here and in eternity, we need to get serious with its Source.

Have you found the Source of everlasting JOY?

If so, have you shared Him with someone?

"You give him blessings forever;
You cheer him with joy in Your presence.
For the king relies on the LORD;
through the faithful love of the Most High
he is not shaken."

King David
Psalm 21:6

4

Universal Peace and Rest

According to a study of 1,300 NDE's from around the world, one of the core elements of the afterlife experience from those researched was "intense and generally positive emotions or feeling (76.2% 'incredible peace')".[1]

I've been a huge Beatles fan since the '60s. As a young guitarist, I learned to play many of their songs. As a teenager, I wore my peace symbol necklace to school. We all wanted world peace. We still do.

John Lennon sang about it in his songs "Give Peace a Chance" and "Imagine." And though he imagined there was no Heaven or hell – something Jesus taught DID exist – Lennon expressed a deep longing for peace that's shared by everyone.

Well, if you like universal peace, you'll LOVE God's Heaven, and the New Earth that is promised (Isaiah 65:17, as quoted in the Introduction).

About 700 years before Christ was born in Bethlehem, the prophet Isaiah wrote:

"For a child will be born for us, a son will be given to us, and the government will be on His shoulders. He will be named Wonderful Counselor, Mighty God, Eternal Father, Prince of Peace" (Isaiah 9:6).

True lasting peace will come only by the Prince of Peace – Jesus Christ. Consider these truths about Peace:

"You will keep the mind that is dependent on You in perfect peace, for it is trusting in You" (Isaiah 26:3).

"Lord, You will establish peace for us, for You have also done all our work for us" (Isaiah 26:12).

"The Lord gives His people strength; the Lord blesses His people with peace" (Psalm 29:11).

And this is one of my all-time favorite promises from God about peace:

"If only you had paid attention to My commands. Then your peace would have been like a river, and your righteousness like the waves of the sea" (Isaiah 48:18).

Imagine sitting on the bank of a quiet river. There's something incredibly calming and serene about a peaceful river.

Jesus said, "Peace I leave with you. My peace I give to you. I do not give to you as the world gives. Your heart must not be troubled or fearful" (John 14:27).

Notice that His peace is not "as the world gives." The world's peace is temporary and superficial; it lasts only until the next struggle or war begins. Throughout history, somewhere in the world, there have been wars or conflicts.

The United Nations claims world peace as one of its goals.

But since its founding in 1945, there's not been world peace. Why? By ourselves, mankind cannot bring world peace because we are flawed. Again, only the Prince of Peace – Jesus Christ can do that.

The key to true peace and rest is a righteous life. "He will enter into peace— they will rest on their beds— everyone who lives uprightly" (Isaiah 57:2).

The apostle Paul wrote, "For those who live according to the flesh think about the things of the flesh, but those who live according to the Spirit, about the things of the Spirit. For the mind-set of the flesh is death, but the mind-set of the Spirit is life and *peace*" (Romans 8:5-6, emphasis mine).

***

Rest. What a beautiful word.

What comes to mind when you think of resting? Sleeping in late? Napping in a hammock strung up between two palm trees? Curling up with the one you love on a sofa by a warm fire?

Whatever it is, God's rest is absolutely the most restful. After all, he invented it.

"By the seventh day God completed His work that He had done, and He rested on the seventh day from all His work that He had done" (Genesis 2:2).

Rest even made it into the Ten Commandments (both First AND Second Editions, since Moses busted the first one).

(1st ed.) "Remember the Sabbath day, to keep it holy: You are to labor six days and do all your work, but the seventh day is a Sabbath to the LORD your God. You must not do any work—you, your son or daughter, your male or female slave, your livestock, or the foreigner who is within your gates.

"For the LORD made the heavens and the earth, the sea, and everything in them in six days; then He rested on the seventh day.

"Therefore the LORD blessed the Sabbath day and declared it holy" (Exodus 20:11).

(2nd ed.) "You are to labor six days but you must rest on the seventh day…" (Exodus 34:21).

In fact, the word "Sabbath" comes from the Hebrew word "שׁבת" (Shabat), meaning "cessation" or "time of rest."

Jesus said, "Come to Me, all of you who are weary and burdened, and I will give you rest. All of you, take up My yoke and learn from Me, because I am gentle and humble in heart, and you will find rest for yourselves. For My yoke is easy and My burden is light" (Matthew 11:28-30).

Rest is necessary to recharge our batteries, to let our body heal, to regain strength. And only in Heaven will we find our eternal rest... in peace... forever.
R.I.P.

Would you like real peace while on Earth, and eternal peace and rest in Heaven?

Do you know someone else who does?

"Peace I leave with you.
My peace I give to you.
I do not give to you as the world gives.
Your heart must not be troubled or fearful."

Jesus Christ
John 14:27

5

Our Ultimate Hope

When you hear all the bad news around the world, the country, or your local area, does it seem that the world has no hope?

Do you ever feel hopeless? In what have you placed your hope?

Your "lucky star"?

A political party or politician?

A friend or spouse?

A retirement account (if you have one)?

Yourself?

Nothing in this world can provide hope. False hopes will let you down. But Heaven provides a "living hope." One that is absolutely guaranteed. In fact, as a Christian, this hope is *reserved* for you, in Jesus Christ.

Paul wrote to the believers in Colossae:

"We always thank God, the Father of our Lord Jesus Christ, when we pray for you, for we have heard of your faith in Christ Jesus and of the love you have for all the saints because of the hope reserved for you in heaven. You have already heard about this hope in the message of truth, the gospel that has come to you. It is bearing fruit and growing all over the world, just as it has among you since the day you heard it and recognized God's grace in the truth" (Colossians 1:3-6).

Peter the fisherman, in a moment of weakness, blew it by denying he was a disciple of Jesus when Jesus was arrested. But, he was restored to this hope. He confessed:

"Praise the God and Father of our Lord Jesus Christ. According to His great mercy, He has given us a new birth into a living hope through the resurrection of Jesus Christ from the dead and into an inheritance that is imperishable, uncorrupted, and unfading, kept in heaven for you" (1 Peter 1:3-4).

That's an amazing hope and inheritance, made possible with "a new birth." Yes, as Jesus said, we "must be born again." Read chapter 3 in the Book of John.

Mark Buchanan, in his excellent book *Things Unseen – Living in Light of Forever*, writes, "Like the tug and heft of a huge unseen planet hovering near, the hope of heaven is meant to exert a gravitational pull that gives our lives stability, substance, weight."[1]

We could all use some stability in life, couldn't we? This "hope of heaven" pulls us out of the despair and hopelessness of this world and toward real life, real hope, and real love.

It boggles my mind to realize that the Creator of the universe wants to fill us to overflowing with love, joy, peace... and hope. It's possible only through His Holy Spirit, indwelling us when we place our faith in Him.

"'For I know the plans I have for you' — this is the LORD's declaration — 'plans for your welfare, not for disaster, to give you a future and a hope'" (Jeremiah 29:11).

Apostle Paul said:

"Now may the God of hope fill you with all joy and peace as you believe in Him so that you may overflow with hope by the power of the Holy Spirit" (Romans 15:13).

Read Colossians 1:3-6 again, at the beginning of this chapter.

So, where does "the hope reserved for you in heaven" come from? It comes in the "message of truth, the gospel that has come to you."

"Gospel" simply means "good news."

Just think - the gospel message of Jesus Christ, originating around 33 A.D., has survived centuries of time, and made it all the way to you and me today.

But there's one magnificent event, yet to come, that provides me and billions of people the strongest source of hope. It's our "blessed hope," the most comforting assurance of lasting world peace and personal joy forever...

Jesus Christ is returning to Earth.

(this is worth repeating...)

JESUS CHRIST is returning to Earth!!

Why?

He's coming back to be with His bride – the universal Church (true believers), and to set up His kingdom of love and peace forever.

How do I know? He said so Himself...

"If I go away and prepare a place for you, I will come back and receive you to Myself, so that where I am you may be also" (John 14:3).

"For as the lightning comes from the east and flashes as far as the west, so will be the coming of the Son of Man" (Matthew 24:27).

The Bible has over one hundred verses on this topic.

Luke, the physician who accompanied Apostle Paul on his journeys, recorded what the "two men dressed in white" (angels) said while the disciples watched Jesus ascend into Heaven from the Mount of Olives, a few weeks after His resurrection:

"They said, 'Men of Galilee, why do you stand looking up into heaven? This Jesus, who has been taken from you into heaven, will come in the same way that you have seen Him going into heaven'" (Acts 1:11).

The writer of the book of Hebrews also says:

"...so also the Messiah, having been offered once to bear the sins of many, will appear a second time, not to bear sin, but to bring salvation to those who are waiting for Him" (Hebrews 9:28).

Paul, in his letter to Titus said, "...while we wait for the blessed hope and appearing of the glory of our great God and Savior, Jesus Christ" (Titus 2:13).

In fact, the prophet Zechariah predicts exactly where He will first touch Earth when He returns – exactly the same place He ascended from:

"Then the LORD will go out to fight against those nations as He fights on a day of battle. On that day, His feet will stand on the Mount of Olives, which faces Jerusalem on the east. The Mount of Olives will be split in half from east to west, forming a huge valley, so that half the mountain will move to the north and half to the south" (Zechariah 14:3-4).

Interestingly, in 1964 while a location for the Hotel of the Seven Arches was being considered, an earthquake fault line was discovered running east to west, right through the Mount of Olives.[2]

Are *you* eagerly waiting for His return? Or are you hoping it's not true? I am *so glad* I've placed all my hope in Jesus. It helps me get through each day, no matter what comes my way. And this "blessed hope" is not only for our present life, but for *eternity*.

I like how Apostle Paul put it:
"If we have put our hope in Christ for this life only, we should be pitied more than anyone" (1 Corinthians 15:19).

Have *you* believed God's good news, including the return of Christ, for your ultimate hope?

Do you know someone who could use some hope?

"Hope, like the gleaming taper's light,
Adorns and cheers our way;
And still, as darker grows the night,
Emits a brighter ray."

Oliver Goldsmith (1728 – 1774)

6

Forgiveness

Have you ever felt guilty for doing or thinking something that deep down you knew was wrong?

Have you ever tried to deny guilty feelings?

Do you ever feel like a weight of guilt and condemnation is following you around like a dark cloud?

Do you sense a still, small voice within you trying to guide you in the right way?

I'm pretty sure we *all* "hear" voices in our head at certain times or situations. One voice may prompt us to talk to someone who's hurting. Another voice may accuse us of being no good, or a failure, or hopeless. We all have a conscience... but we can choose whether to heed it or ignore it. The more we heed it, the easier it is to "hear" it. The more we ignore it, the harder it is for us to "hear" it.

Our individual conscience is a God-given instrument – a compass – to help us make right decisions. It is especially powerful when, by faith, the Spirit of Jesus enables our conscience to guide us to follow His will.

When our conscience is feeling guilty about something we've done or said, we should seek forgiveness from the one we offended, whether it's a person or God. And though a few people may find it difficult to forgive, you can rest assured that the God of Heaven is eager to do so.

Charles Spurgeon (1834-1892), the great British preacher, compared God's forgiveness to what Noah saw: "The floods of grace prevail above the mountains of our sins. Almighty love paints a rainbow on the blackest clouds of human transgression."[1]

Nothing that you or I have done or said is beyond eternal forgiveness, as long as we simply accept it. However, if we reject forgiveness, there's nothing to help us escape eternal separation from God. We have the power to choose.

When we find the gift of forgiveness in Jesus Christ, we can kiss guilt goodbye... forever!

Some of us have more to be forgiven of than others, but we all need it. If I say I have no sin, I'm calling God a liar, which is a sin.

The apostle John wrote:

If we say, "We have no sin," then we are deceiving ourselves and the truth is not in us. If we confess our sins, He is faithful and righteous to forgive us our sins and to cleanse us from all unrighteousness. If we say, "We don't have any sin," we make Him a liar, and His word is not in us (1 John 1:8-10).

Picture this scene of Jesus dining with a "righteous" man, when a woman (of shady past) arrives:

Then one of the Pharisees invited Him to eat with him. He entered the Pharisee's house and reclined at the table. And a woman in the town who was a sinner found out that Jesus was reclining at the table in the Pharisee's house. She brought an alabaster jar of fragrant oil and stood behind Him at His feet, weeping, and began to wash His feet with her tears. She wiped His feet with the hair of her head, kissing them and anointing them with the fragrant oil.

When the Pharisee who had invited Him saw this, he said to himself, "This man, if He were a prophet, would know who and what kind of woman this is who is touching Him — she's a sinner!"

Jesus replied to him, "Simon, I have something to say to you."

"Teacher," he said, "say it."

"A creditor had two debtors. One owed 500 denarii, and the other 50. Since they could not pay it back, he graciously forgave them both. So, which of them will love him more?"

Simon answered, "I suppose the one he forgave more."

"You have judged correctly," He told him. Turning to the woman, He said to Simon, "Do you see this woman? I entered your house; you gave Me no water for My feet, but she, with her tears, has washed My feet and wiped them with her hair. You gave Me no kiss, but she hasn't stopped kissing My feet since I came in. You didn't anoint My head with olive oil, but she has anointed My feet with fragrant oil. Therefore I tell you, her many sins have been forgiven; that's why she loved much. But the one who is forgiven little, loves little." Then He said to her, "Your sins are forgiven."

Those who were at the table with Him began to say among themselves, "Who is this man who even forgives sins?"

And He said to the woman, "Your faith has saved you. Go in peace" (Luke 7:36-50).

There's nothing like the peace that comes through forgiveness. And in Heaven, both will last forever.

Ian McCormack, the young man who had an NDE after a deadly sting from a box jellyfish (see Chapter 2), had this to say about being in God's presence and forgiveness:

"I proceeded to tell him [God] about all the disgusting things I'd done under the cover of darkness. But it was as though He'd already forgiven me and the intensity of His love only increased. In fact, later God showed me that when I'd asked for forgiveness in the ambulance, it was then that He forgave me and washed my spirit clean from evil."[2]

Forgiveness is like being washed clean – forever. So, to know Jesus is to know forgiveness (or love, or peace, or hope, or any of the other desires we have).

No Jesus, no forgiveness.

Here's some more food for thought:

Jesus said, "I assure you: *anyone* who hears My Word and believes Him who sent Me has eternal life and *will not* come under judgment but *has passed* from death to life" (John 5:24, emphasis mine).

"And forgive us our sins, for we ourselves also forgive everyone in debt to us" (Luke 11:4).

Paul, the apostle, wrote to the believers in Rome, "Therefore, no condemnation now exists for those in Christ Jesus" (Romans 8:1).

"So then, as through one trespass there is condemnation for everyone, so also through one righteous act there is life-giving justification for everyone. For just as through one man's disobedience [Adam] the many were made sinners, so also through the one man's obedience [Jesus] the many will be made righteous. The law came along to multiply the trespass. But where sin multiplied, grace multiplied even more so that, just as sin reigned in death, so also grace will reign through righteousness, resulting in eternal life through Jesus Christ our Lord" (Romans 5:18-21).

"Come, let us discuss this," says the LORD. "Though your sins are like scarlet, they will be as white as snow; though they are as red as crimson, they will be like wool" (Isaiah 1:18).

"My little children, I am writing you these things so that you may not sin. But if anyone does sin, we have an advocate with the Father — Jesus Christ the Righteous One. He Himself is the propitiation [substitutionary payment] for our sins, and not only for ours, but also for those of the whole world" (1 John 2:1-2).

The punishment for our sins was placed on Jesus, who willingly took our place. He paid the debt that we owed, but had no way of paying.

Here on Earth, you and I can begin to experience forgiveness through faith in Jesus.

But in Heaven, we'll enjoy forgiveness *for eternity*...with our Forgiver.

Could you use some forgiveness in this life, and the life to come?

Is there someone you should forgive?

Since God promises to forgive us,
we must also forgive ourselves...no matter
what we've done.
By not forgiving myself, am I not establishing
myself as a judge more superior
than Him?

Heaven is...

7

Freedom

In 1969, Richie Havens sang about "Freedom" at the Woodstock music festival. I was only thirteen. I heard it on the radio, and the thought of yearning to be free entered my young mind then, but I was too young to really understand what it was all about.

History is replete with people wanting to be free:

- the Israelites wanted freedom from Pharaoh (abt 1500 B.C.)
- William Wallace and the Scots wanted freedom from a power-hungry King Edward (1297 A.D.)
- black slaves in Africa wanted freedom from their black owners (throughout the history of Africa)
- Christians sought religious freedom in the New World (17th century)
- Many in the American colonies yearned for freedom from the tyrannical King George in England (1776)
- Many black slaves in America wanted freedom from their white owners (18th century)

- the Jews in Europe during WWII wanted freedom from Hitler (1930s - 1945)
- the prisoner behind bars wants to be set free

You can probably think of others.

Just what is freedom?

Doing whatever you want whenever you want? Going wherever you want to go? Having no one telling you what to do? That's partly right, but it's much more than that.

One thing is for sure: every person longs for it.

As our Creator has revealed to us in His Word, true freedom lies not in the ability to do *anything* you want, anytime and anywhere, but rather in the ability to do the *right* thing, every time and everywhere, without being enslaved by our own wrong and selfish desires.

Religion professor Albert Wolters, in *Creation Regained,* writes, "Jesus' miracles provide us with a sample of the meaning of redemption: a freeing of creation from the shackles of sin and evil and a reinstatement of creaturely living as intended by God."[1] Before the fall of mankind in the Garden of Eden, the whole creation was free from "sin and evil." But since the willful disobedience of Adam and Eve, all of creation has been subject to (a slave to) sin and evil.

But Jesus, through His death, burial, and resurrection, has provided the first step to complete freedom for all of creation – humans, animals, the Earth - which will find its complete fulfillment in the New Earth that is promised.

Apostle Paul wrote:

"Christ has liberated us to be free. Stand firm then and don't submit again to a yoke of slavery" (Galatians 5:1).

He's teaching us that, as believers in Christ, we're no longer under Law but under Grace. The Christian life on earth is not trying to live up to a bunch of do's and don'ts, but living a victorious life in the power of His Spirit. To the believers in Corinth, Paul wrote:

"Now the Lord is the Spirit, and where the Spirit of the Lord is, there is freedom" (2 Corinthians 3:17).

Again, Paul writes, "Therefore, no condemnation now exists for those in Christ Jesus, because the Spirit's law of life in Christ Jesus has set you free from the law of sin and of death" (Romans 8:1-2).

What makes us free? Truth.

Here's how John the apostle put it:

"As He was saying these things, many believed in Him. So Jesus said to the Jews who had believed Him, 'If you continue in My Word, you really are My disciples. You will know the truth, and the truth will set you free.'

"'We are descendants of Abraham,' they answered Him, 'and we have never been enslaved to anyone. How can you say, 'You will become free'?

"Jesus responded, 'I assure you: Everyone who commits sin is a slave of sin. A slave does not remain in the household forever, but a son does remain forever. Therefore, if the Son sets you free, you really will be free'" (John 8:30-36).

He also claimed, "I am the way, the truth, and the life. No one comes to the Father except through me" (John 14:6).

Where do we find truth? In knowing and following Jesus. He IS truth.

What does it mean that "the truth shall set you free"?

Truth brings freedom. Truth and Freedom must therefore be interconnected. We cannot have ultimate freedom without knowing truth.

Lies lead to slavery. For example:

- the lie that alcohol, drugs, money, pornography, or a thousand other worldly temptations, will make you happy and fulfilled, only leads to addiction and greed and enslavement to our weaknesses.

- the lie that big government is here to help you, leads to dependence (slavery).

- the lie that some people are not as valuable as others leads to abuse, hatred, abortion, euthanasia, and concentration camps.

- the lie that "there is no absolute truth" (which itself seems rather absolute) only leads to moral confusion and vulnerability to more lies.

On the other hand:

- The *truth* that God created you in His image brings priceless value to you, and the freedom to be who He made you to be.

- The *truth* that your Creator loves you gives you a reason to live.

- The *truth* that Jesus Christ took our sins upon Himself and died in our place brings release from sin's bondage.

- The *truth* that He rose from the dead three days later and ascended into Heaven until His return gives us hope beyond measure that there's another world waiting for His followers.

Only Truth brings Freedom.
Truth is a Person...
Jesus Christ.

Is there a substance or habit to which you feel enslaved?

Have *you* found the Truth Who brings the everlasting freedom you yearn for?

"To obey God is freedom."

Seneca the Younger (5? B.C. – A.D. 65)

Heaven is...

8

Paradise Beyond Nature

What does Paradise look like to you?

For me, I think of a warm tropical island beach, or a beautiful, quiet valley full of lush green foliage, huge trees, and colorful flowers. Others may envision mountain views, or gentle rolling hills, or something else altogether.

Those are all nice, but are only a small taste, I believe, of what Jesus invites us to.

Since the '60s, there's been a growing movement to clean up and conserve nature around us. Just like cleaning your room when you were young, or picking up litter along a highway, it's always good to restore order and purity to our home and environment. There seems to be something in all of us that yearns for paradise.

While Jesus was on the cross dying, two thieves who were crucified with Him had a few last words to say...and one was promised paradise by our dying Savior:

"Then one of the criminals hanging there began to yell insults at Him: 'Aren't You the Messiah? Save Yourself and us!' But the other answered, rebuking him: 'Don't you even fear God, since you are undergoing the same punishment? We are punished justly, because we're getting back what we deserve for the things we did, but this man has done nothing wrong.' Then he said, "Jesus, remember me when You come into Your kingdom!'

"And He said to him, 'I assure you: Today you will be with Me in paradise'" (Luke 23:39-43).

And that thief who believed is STILL in paradise! Can you imagine Jesus Christ saying the same thing to you?

If you have believed in Him, He did.
"[put your name here], I assure you: [when you die] you will be with Me in paradise!"

He died for all. His invitation to Paradise is for all.

But what is "paradise" like?
Merriam-Webster dictionary defines it as: "a very beautiful, pleasant, or peaceful place that seems to be perfect"...and "a place or state of bliss, felicity, or delight."

Who wouldn't want that? Especially if it's eternal AND in the presence of the Creator of the universe!

I love to read anything by C. S. Lewis, the atheist-turned-Christian author and Oxford professor. His comment about going "beyond Nature" is one of my favorite things to think about. He wrote, "Nature is mortal; we shall outlive her. When all the suns and nebulae have passed away, each one of you will still be alive.

"Nature is only the image, the symbol; but it is the symbol Scripture invites me to use.

"We are summoned to pass in through Nature, beyond her, into that splendor which she fitfully reflects. And in there, in beyond Nature, we shall eat of the tree of life."[1]

There is an invisible world "beyond Nature" that Jesus offers to His followers. The beautiful nature we see now is only a type, an earthly model of what's in store for those who have received Jesus as their Savior.

Whenever people who've had an NDE speak of their visit to what they believe was Heaven - "beyond Nature" - they describe the colors of the scenery as being immensely more vivid, bright, and translucent than anything seen on Earth... and a multitude *more* colors than we can see with our physical eyes.[2]

Dale Black, who had an NDE when his plane crashed, described the colors as so alive that they quivered and throbbed with vitality.[3]

We learned in science class that colors come from the light spectrum. The apostle James gave God an intriguing name when he wrote:

"Every generous act and every perfect gift is from above, coming down from the Father of lights; with Him there is no variation or shadow cast by turning" (James 1:17).

God is the "Father of lights" because He spoke light into existence.
"Then God said, 'Let there be light,' and there was light" (Genesis 1:3).

It follows, then, that in Heaven there will be an abundance of light and colors to enjoy... forever.

Not only are the glimpses of "beyond nature" which are seen by NDErs indescribably beautiful, but so will be the New Earth that is coming. And its beauty will have a familiarity to it because it will resemble creation we now see, but with a much grander and deeper beauty.

The prophet Isaiah wrote about the new Earth:

- "The wilderness and the dry land will be glad; the desert will rejoice and blossom like a rose" (Isaiah 35:1).

- "For the LORD will comfort Zion;
He will comfort all her waste places,
and He will make her wilderness like
Eden, and her desert like the garden of
the LORD. Joy and gladness will be found
in her, thanksgiving and melodious song"
(Isaiah 51:3).

- "Instead of the thornbush, a cypress will come up, and instead of the brier, a myrtle will come up; it will make a name for Yahweh as an everlasting sign that will not be destroyed" (Isaiah 55:13).

Would you like to live in Paradise...forever?

Do you know someone else who would?

"Anyone who has an ear should listen to what the
Spirit says to the churches. I will give the victor the
right to eat from the tree of life,
which is in God's
paradise."

Jesus Christ
Revelation 2:7

9

Filled with the Best Music

Like many of you reading this book, I grew up around music, because it's in my heritage.

One of my grandfathers played horns and led a big band in the '30s called Sandy's Rhythm Band. They played gigs in Indiana. An uncle played saxophone in that band and also soloed professionally. My grandmother was a church organist and pianist. My parents both loved singing and my mother was a church choir director. One of my brothers plays guitar and fiddle in a bluegrass band, another brother played bass guitar for many years, and my oldest brother can't carry a... well, let's just say the music gene completely bypassed him.

I picked up guitar at age eleven and during high school in the early '70s was in a garage rock band that even had paying gigs during the summers. Since then, I've enjoyed learning classical guitar and fingerstyle (e.g., James Taylor and Hawaiian slack key), performed at weddings, and even sang in a barbershop quartet. I've held three jobs in music radio in the past and I now teach guitar lessons on the side.

Do you like to listen to music? Is there a song that speaks to your soul or makes you want to dance?

Do you enjoy different styles of music or just one?

Music is the universal language. It's the language of our spirit. And just as there are many varieties of animals, plants, trees, flowers, insects, snowflakes, and stars in our world (exhibiting the creativity of God), so there are many styles of music (showing the creativity of humans) that appeal to different people.

Martin Luther said, "Next to the Word of God, the noble art of music is the greatest treasure in the world."

God, being the Creator of all things, is the source of mankind's talent for writing, composing, and playing music.

As a musician, I owe my ability to the One who "knit me together in my mother's womb" (Psalm 139:13). The same Creator who "trains my hands for battle, and my fingers for warfare" (Psalm 144:1), also grants musical ability to various ones as He desires.

King David, the warrior and musician, exclaimed:

Hallelujah! Sing to the LORD a new song,
His praise in the assembly of the godly.
Let Israel celebrate its Maker; let the children of Zion rejoice in their King.
Let them praise His name with dancing
and make music to Him with tambourine and lyre (Psalm 149:1-3).

My favorite classical composer, Johann Sebastian Bach (1685-1750) said, "All music should be written for the glorification of God and for the permissible delectation of the mind."
He and George Frederick Handel inscribed many of their compositions with, "Soli Deo Gloria" – "for the glory of God alone" (sometimes abbreviating it "S.D.G."). This is fitting, since God is the source of music – harmony, rhythm, melody, and lyric. Without God's creative ability forming man in His image, and forming man's intellectual capacity to compose music, we would not have any music, or anything else that has been imagined in the minds of men and women. This includes paintings, sculptures, architecture, machinery, computers, software, robots, space rockets, satellites, or *anything* we create with our minds and hands.

The prophet Isaiah encourages the people of God that in His kingdom, all creation will sing:

"You will indeed go out with joy and be peacefully guided; the mountains and the hills will break into singing before you, and all the trees of the field will clap their hands" (Isaiah 55:12).

In the Bible, "morning stars" and "sons of God" refer to angelic beings. Angels sang at the creation of the universe:

The book of Job (pronounced like *Jobe*) is rich with ancient wisdom. In it, God asked Job,

"Where were you when I established the earth? Tell Me, if you have understanding. Who fixed its dimensions? Certainly you know! Who stretched a measuring line across it? What supports its foundations? Or who laid its cornerstone *while the morning stars sang together and all the sons of God shouted for joy?*" (Job 38:4-7, emphasis mine).

Don't you wish you could have *heard* that? I do. But, no worries… there'll be plenty more singing and music in Heaven for the Christian to enjoy!

I love *The Chronicles of Narnia,* by C. S. Lewis. In the first of the seven books, the creation of Narnia was accomplished with a song by Aslan, who represents Jesus Christ. In Chapter Nine (titled The Founding of Narnia) in the first book, *The Magician's Nephew,* we read:

"All this time the Lion's song, and his stately prowl, to and fro, backwards and forwards, was going on. What was rather alarming was that at each turn he came a little nearer. Polly was finding the song more and more interesting because she thought she was beginning to see the connection between the music and the things that were happening. When a line of dark firs sprang up on a ridge about a hundred yards away, she felt that they were connected with a series of deep, prolonged notes which the Lion had sung a second before. And when he burst into a rapid series of lighter notes she was not surprised to see primroses suddenly appearing in every direction.

"Thus, with an unspeakable thrill, she felt quite certain that all the things were coming (as she said) 'out of the Lion's head.' When you listened to his song you heard the things he was making up: when you looked around you, you saw them. This was so exciting that she had no time to be afraid."[1]

In the Old Testament book of Zephaniah, the prophet, we learn that God Himself sings over His beloved:

"The LORD thy God in the midst of thee is mighty; he will save, he will rejoice over thee with joy; he will rest in his love, he will joy over thee with singing" (Zephaniah 3:17, KJV).

In Apostle John's vision of Heaven, he found a musical instrument - the trumpet...

"And the seven angels who had the seven trumpets prepared to blow them" (Revelations 8:6).

Wouldn't you think, like me, that there's a bunch of other musical instruments there? And what about choirs? (Revelations 5:9-12).

Captain Dale Black, during his NDE after his small plane crashed also heard the most alluring and captivating music. It was omnipresent. It seemed to draw him to the point of actually being one of the instruments. He was full of ecstasy and fascination, adoration and love. He never wanted to leave.[2]

Have you ever experienced a concert or conference that you didn't want to end? For Christians who find joy in worshipping the Creator, some of these events are like a taste of Heaven.

I recently attended a three-day music conference like that in Nashville, Tennessee, put on by an Irish couple, Keith and Kristyn Getty (www.gettymusic.com).

There's currently a growing movement to deepen the spiritual worship in churches by returning to meaningful, congregational singing. The Gettys are an integral part of that movement. If the pure joy and love I felt during the conference music is a taste of Heaven, I cannot wait to hear and feel what's in store for believers in the presence of God![3]

Would you like to enjoy the most beautiful music forever?

Do you know someone else who would?

"Praise Him with trumpet blast;
praise Him with harp and lyre.
Praise Him with tambourine and dance;
praise Him with flute and strings.
Praise Him with resounding cymbals;
praise Him with clashing cymbals.
Let everything that breathes praise the LORD.
Hallelujah!"

King David
(Psalm 150:3-6)

Heaven is...

10

Feasting on the Best Meals

Do you enjoy eating delicious meals, lovingly prepared and shared with family and friends, without worrying about whether it's fattening or not?

How about *free* food?

Then, you'll love Heaven!

In the book of Isaiah, God promises that HE will fulfill your thirst and hunger with Himself:

"Come, everyone who is thirsty, come to the waters; and you without money, come, buy, and eat! Come, buy wine and milk without money and without cost! Why do you spend money on what is not food, and your wages on what does not satisfy? Listen carefully to Me, and eat what is good, and you will enjoy the choicest of foods. Pay attention and come to Me; listen, so that you will live. I will make an everlasting covenant with you, the promises assured to David" (Isaiah 55:1-3).

This is not just good food; it's the "choicest of foods." It truly satisfies our hunger and thirst, not temporarily, but forever.

The apostle John, in describing his vision of heaven while exiled on the island of Patmos, wrote:

"Then I heard something like the voice of a vast multitude, like the sound of cascading waters, and like the rumbling of loud thunder, saying:

'Hallelujah, because our Lord God, the Almighty, has begun to reign! Let us be glad, rejoice, and give Him glory, because the marriage of the Lamb has come, and His wife has prepared herself. She was given fine linen to wear, bright and pure. For the fine linen represents the righteous acts of the saints.' Then he said to me, 'Write: Those invited to the marriage feast of the Lamb are fortunate!' He also said to me, 'These words of God are true'" (Revelation 16:6-9).

That's one marriage feast you won't want to miss!

David, the brave shepherd boy who became King of the united kingdoms of Israel and Judah wrote:

"You prepare a table before me in the presence of my enemies; You anoint my head with oil; my cup overflows" (Psalm 23:5).

Imagine a nice sit-down dinner prepared for you by your mother, or father, or by the First Lady, or a king or queen. These would all be very special, but *nothing* compared to one being prepared by the God of Heaven, the Creator of the universe, by Jesus – the King of kings and Lord of lords!

Consider these verses on eating and drinking in the Kingdom of Heaven:

"I bestow on you a kingdom, just as My Father bestowed one on Me, so that you may eat and drink at My table in My kingdom" (Luke 22:29-30).

"The LORD of Hosts will prepare a feast for all the peoples on this mountain — a feast of aged wine, choice meat, finely aged wine" (Isaiah 25:6).

"When one of those who reclined at the table with Him heard these things, he said to Him, 'The one who will eat bread in the kingdom of God is blessed!'" (Luke 14:15).

"Then he showed me the river of living water, sparkling like crystal, flowing from the throne of God and of the Lamb down the middle of the broad street of the city. The tree of life was on both sides of the river, bearing 12 kinds of fruit, producing its fruit every month. The leaves of the tree are for healing the nations, and there will no longer be any curse..." (Revelation 22:1-3a).

Fruit, wine, choice meats, feasting... sounds like there will be no lack of fine dining in Heaven and on the New Earth! You can bank on it because God Himself, in His Word, has promised it. Not only that, He will be the Chef!

Have you accepted God's invitation to the marriage feast of the Lamb of God?

Do you know someone who is thirsty or hungry for real food that truly satisfies?

"Listen! I stand at the door and knock.
If anyone hears My voice and opens the door,
I will come in to him and have dinner with him, and
he with Me."

Jesus Christ
Revelation 3:20

11

Having Superpowers

Why are there so many movies and books and comic books about humans with superpowers?

I recently saw a woman wearing a t-shirt that said, "I'm a Mom – what's YOUR superpower?"

Truth. Motherhood - and Fatherhood - take a special strength and wisdom.

What superpower, if any, would you like to have?

- to disappear and reappear anywhere?
- to travel great distances instantaneously?
- to learn and retain deep knowledge of things in the universe?
- enhanced vision?
- to control inanimate objects/the weather?
- any others?

Jesus Christ had superpowers here on Earth. In addition to his many miracles of:

- healing the sick and lame (Matthew 14:14)
- creating a feast out of a couple servings of bread and fish (Mark 6:30-44)

- walking on water (Mark 6:45-50)
- commanding a storm to cease (Luke 8:22-25)
- transfiguring Himself into a being of glorious light, with Moses and Elijah suddenly appearing with Him, while three disciples watched in amazement (Matthew 17:1-13)
- raising the dead to life (John 11)

He demonstrated some pretty cool superpowers *after* he was resurrected from his own cruel death.

For example, Cleopas, a follower of Christ, saw Him disappear right in front of his eyes, immediately after realizing it was Jesus he was talking with. Luke records this encounter:

> "He said to them, 'How unwise and slow you are to believe in your hearts all that the prophets have spoken! Didn't the Messiah have to suffer these things and enter into His glory?' Then beginning with Moses and all the Prophets, He interpreted for them the things concerning Himself in all the Scriptures.
>
> "They came near the village where they were going, and He gave the impression that He was going farther. But they urged Him: 'Stay with us, because it's almost evening, and now the day is almost over.' So He went in to stay with them.
>
> "It was as He reclined at the table with them that He took the bread, blessed and broke it, and gave it to them. Then their eyes were opened, and they recognized Him, but He disappeared from their sight. So they said to each other, 'Weren't our hearts

ablaze within us while He was talking with us on the road and explaining the Scriptures to us?' That very hour they got up and returned to Jerusalem. They found the Eleven and those with them gathered together, who said, 'The Lord has certainly been raised, and has appeared to Simon!' Then they began to describe what had happened on the road and how He was made known to them in the breaking of the bread" (Luke 24:25-35).

He could also walk through walls and suddenly appear out of nowhere. He did this twice within eight days. John 20:19-30 says:

> "In the evening of that first day of the week, the disciples were gathered together with the doors locked because of their fear of the Jews. Then Jesus came, stood among them, and said to them, 'Peace to you!'
> Having said this, He showed them His hands and His side. So the disciples rejoiced when they saw the Lord.
> Jesus said to them again, 'Peace to you! As the Father has sent Me, I also send you.' After saying this, He breathed on them and said, 'Receive the Holy Spirit. If you forgive the sins of any, they are forgiven them; if you retain the sins of any, they are retained.'
> But one of the Twelve, Thomas (called "Twin"), was not with them when Jesus came. So the other disciples kept telling him, 'We have seen the Lord!'

"But he said to them, 'If I don't see the mark of the nails in His hands, put my finger into the mark of the nails, and put my hand into His side, I will never believe!'

"After eight days His disciples were indoors again, and Thomas was with them. Even though the doors were locked, Jesus came and stood among them. He said, 'Peace to you!'

"Then He said to Thomas, 'Put your finger here and observe My hands. Reach out your hand and put it into My side. Don't be an unbeliever, but a believer.'

"Thomas responded to Him, 'My Lord and my God!'

"Jesus said, 'Because you have seen Me, you have believed. Those who believe without seeing are blessed.'

"Jesus performed many other signs in the presence of His disciples that are not written in this book. But these are written so that you may believe Jesus is the Messiah, the Son of God, and by believing you may have life in His name."

Here's another superpower we'll have: travel at the speed of light.

For people in our day who have had a near-death experience, many share a common experience of being able to travel great distances very quickly. Howard Storm shares his story in his book "*My Descent into Death: A Second Chance at Life*":

"We rose upward, gradually at first, and then like a rocket we shot out of that dark and detestable hell. We traversed an enormous distance, light-years, although very little time elapsed..."[1]

Can you imagine that kind of ability to move from one place to another? No rocket built by man can equal that, nor will there ever be.

How about the superpower of comprehending things that you never thought possible?

Do you enjoy learning new things? Have you ever thought, especially while in school, that "my brain is full"? Or do you have trouble remembering things you should already know?

Jesus already invited us to "learn from Me" (Matthew 11:29). Wouldn't He continue that invitation in Heaven? I believe He will.

Heaven will be an *eternity* of new experiences and of learning about the universe and its Creator. And you'll have a perfect memory! Apostle Paul writes that God will show us many things over time:

"Together with Christ Jesus He also raised us up and seated us in the heavens, so that *in the coming ages He might display* the immeasurable riches of His grace through His kindness to us in Christ Jesus" (Ephesians 2:6-7, emphasis mine).

George Ritchie, during his NDE, shares how in Heaven he experienced an ability to learn and discover new things unimaginable here on Earth. There were magnificent structures and buildings of what appeared to be universities, including a library the size of an entire college campus.[2]

Enhanced vision is another superpower I believe Christians in Heaven will have. No more nearsightedness, farsightedness, cataracts, "floaties," lazy eye, blindness, or any other vision problem. Instead, we'll have the ability to see more vividly, and with additional powers.

"Dr. Long notes that 66 percent of NDErs he surveyed describe vision as a heightened, unworldly brightness, clarity, and vividness. Some described a 360-degree vision, others the ability to 'telescope' to long distances and see things far away up close."[3]

Let's bring it back down to Earth for a moment. In actuality, Christ's followers today already have some superpowers that can be exercised daily:

- **Answered Prayer/Moving Mountains**
  - o "I assure you: If anyone says to this mountain, 'Be lifted up and thrown into the sea,' and does not doubt in his heart, but believes that what he says will happen, it will be done for him. Therefore I tell you, all the things you pray and ask for—believe that you have received them, and you will have them" (Mark 11:23-24).

- o "You ask and don't receive because you ask with
  wrong motives, so that you may spend it on
  your evil desires" (James 4:3).

- **Resisting Evil (the "dark side")**
  - o "Finally, be strengthened by the Lord and by His
    vast strength. Put on the full armor of God so
    that you can stand against the tactics of the
    devil. For our battle is not against flesh and
    blood, but against the rulers, against the
    authorities, against the world powers of this
    darkness, against the spiritual forces of evil in
    the heavens. This is why you must take up the
    full armor of God, so that you may be able to
    resist in the evil day, and having prepared
    everything, to take your stand. Stand, therefore,
    with truth like a belt around your waist,
    righteousness like armor on your chest, and your
    feet sandaled with readiness for the gospel of
    peace. In every situation take the shield of faith,
    and with it you will be able to extinguish all the
    flaming arrows of the evil one. Take the
    helmet of salvation, and the sword of the Spirit,
    which is God's Word" (Ephesians 6:10-17).

- **Miracles**
  - o "I assure you: The one who believes in Me will
    also do the works that I do. And he will do even

greater works than these, because I am going to the Father" (John 14:12).

Would you like to have earthly and heavenly super powers?

Have you believed in the only One who can grant them to you?

Now glory be to God,
who by his mighty power at work within us
is able to do far more than we would ever dare to
ask or even dream of—infinitely beyond our
highest prayers, desires, thoughts, or hopes.

Paul the Apostle
Ephesians 3:20
(The Living Bible)

Heaven is...

12

The Best High

Why do some people like to get high or drunk? Curiosity? Loneliness? Peer pressure?

I spent twenty years (1977-1997) in the Navy's Submarine Service. When we visited foreign ports around the world, the first place most of my shipmates visited was the bar. They would get drunk, stumble back to the boat, and pay for it the next day with a hangover, then do it all over again at the next port. I wasn't part of that scene, but *before* the Navy, I had my own way of escaping.

I'll admit it. When I was a teenager during the early '70s, I fell into the drug culture for three years. I'll spare you the details, and share this condensed description of a preacher's kid gone rogue:

My father was a humble Baptist preacher in a small country church and my mother was an elementary school teacher. I first learned about Jesus from them and from Sunday School teachers. In 1968, I decided to believe in Christ and receive Him as my Savior and Lord, and grew spiritually with the help of a Christian math teacher and high school friends in a youth group.

In the early '70s about thirty of us took a three-hour bus ride to Ford's Theater in Washington, D.C. to see "Godspell."

It was awesome! I even sang in a Christian musical production called "Natural High" that we performed at our school.

But I had other friends in school who were getting into marijuana, not Jesus. I wanted to be cool with them, too.

So at 17, while a junior in high school, I allowed other worldly influences into my life, and I gave in to peer pressure and curiosity.

I still remember my younger brother and me trying marijuana for the first time together. Friends at high school were doing it and it was easy to obtain. It felt really cool. It made listening to music, or any activity for that matter, more fun and... "interesting."

Life was becoming nothing more than living for the next high, the next party.

And then one evening in 1974, while riding in my brother's VW van near Williamsburg, Virginia, (where two of my brothers and I lived for a year) my brother and I were minding our own business (which included smoking pot). Suddenly, we were unpleasantly surprised by flashing blue lights behind us. The police told us they had pulled us over because the vehicle was weaving on the road a bit. As they shined their bright flashlights into the van, they caught sight of a marijuana cigarette butt ("roach") in the ashtray. Then they found the rest of my small stash that I had bought.

Yep. We got busted for marijuana possession. That's when our parents found out we smoked pot.

Yep. Bad scene. We were preacher's kids.

My younger brother, who was driving his VW minivan when we got pulled over, got six months' probation (we were still under 18), and I was declared innocent (amazingly).

But that didn't stop us. We just tried to be smarter at it.

But after a while, it began to lose its attraction. I was getting tired of constantly avoiding getting caught, by the police or my parents. I realized it was an empty path. It may have been fun for the moment, but it never lasted.

God, whom I used to follow daily, reading my Bible, praying, enjoying the Jesus music of the early '70s (like Larry Norman) was beginning to draw me back to Him. I began to miss the sweet relationship I had experienced with Jesus.

In 1977, at age 20, I joined the Navy, mainly to gain training in electronics and "see the world." While in boot camp in San Diego, I attended a chapel service and recommitted my life to God. At a bookstore soon afterwards I picked up a book by the late Billy Graham titled *World Aflame*. God used that book to bring me back into fellowship with Him and His plan for my life. It reminded me that I was made for something much more than the next high. The world was full of problems, and I no longer wanted to be a part of the problem, but a part of the solution.

Soon after boot camp, God led me to volunteer for submarine duty. When I got to Naval Submarine School in Groton, Connecticut, it wasn't long before I ran into some Christians who were, well... "high" on Jesus. Two young men, one named Tony, were visiting sailors in my barracks and invited me and others to a weekly Navigators Bible study. I had never heard of The Navigators.[1]

I started going, and I've never been the same since.

These guys (and gals) were definitely high on something, or someone. They smiled and laughed a lot, said "Praise Jesus!" often, memorized and recited Bible verses daily, played a lot of soccer, prayed with energy regularly, and loved telling others of the joy and peace and hope they had found.

It was infectious, and I was so ready to leave the worldly "high" behind for this heavenly one that truly satisfied. I was a prodigal son returning to his Father's love and close relationship.

I began to truly experience this for myself. The closer I got to God through obedience, reading and meditating on His Word, prayer, fellowship, and witnessing to others, the more fulfilled and joyful I became. His Holy Spirit filled me with the fruit of the Spirit - love, joy, peace, patience, kindness, goodness, gentleness, faithfulness and self-control (Galatians 5:22-23).

I had come full circle, back to where I belonged; back to what I was created for.

And I truly believe this spiritual high is just a small taste of the everlasting "high" believers will experience in Heaven.

Those who have had an NDE share a common observation – that life in Heaven will have some familiarity to our current life, but with one major difference: a much higher dimension and intensity. More ecstasy, serenity, and adventure.[2]

More on that "adventure" part in Chapter 17.

Drugs messed me up as a teenager. It became a detriment to my relationships, my work, and my future. But following Jesus rescued me from a meaningless life. He didn't *mess* me up, he *dressed* me up – for an eternal "high."

Would you like to experience an everlasting sense of ecstasy and bliss?

Do you know someone else you'd like to share this "high" with?

"Before,
I was all messed up on drugs,
but since I've found the Lord,
I'm all messed up on the Lord!"

From "Big Bambu", Cheech and Chong
(a comedy duo album I had
during my wayward teenage years)

13

No Pain, Grief, or Death

Every person in the world has known physical pain to some degree. It's part of living in our physical world. You may be experiencing it right now. And there are many forms of painkillers, but they're only temporary in effectiveness, and some are addictive, leading to still more problems.

Grief has no partiality. It strikes all of us at some point, and more than once. Instead of being physical, it is emotional pain, coming from loss of someone you love, or something you cherished, or many other ways.

Death can come slowly, passing through pain and grief first. It can also come suddenly. I'm sure you can think of people in your life who have lived through a long, painful existence as they struggled with disease or infirmity; and others who have died suddenly.

But for the believer, we know God's promise, that one day the blind will see, the deaf will hear, the lame will run, and the mute will talk (see Isaiah 35:5-6) - and it will *all* be worth it. Someone has rightly said, "In light of heaven, the worst suffering on earth, a life full of the most atrocious tortures on earth, will be seen to be no more serious than one night in an inconvenient hotel."[1]

Then again, some people die suddenly. Gary Wood, who had an NDE after a car accident, was pronounced dead, but lived to tell an amazing story of being free from all pain in Heaven, immediately after the accident. Then he met an old friend who had been decapitated in an accident while they were in high school together. His friend was complete and whole. They embraced each other and realized that, since they were in spirit form, their hugs went through their spiritual bodies.[2]

Who wouldn't want to live in a place where there's no pain, grief, or death...forever?! These things are a result of sin, when Adam and Eve disobeyed God in the Garden of Eden.

Doubtless, you and I would have done the same. But, we can read and hear His Word today, and we can choose to obey. God provides the way to escape these curses forever through faith in His Son. Jesus paid our penalty for sin, through His death on the Cross, and His resurrection to Heaven, where He awaits those of us who accept His free gift of forgiveness.

Consider these comforting words from God's Word:

"This has now been made evident through the appearing of our Savior Christ Jesus, who has abolished death and has brought life and immortality to light through the gospel" (2 Timothy 1:10).

"He will wipe away every tear from their eyes. Death will no longer exist; grief, crying, and pain will exist no longer, because the previous things have passed away" (Revelation 21:4).

"The last enemy to be abolished is death" (1 Corinthians 15:26).

The apostle John wrote, "And this is the testimony: God has given us eternal life, and this life is in His Son. The one who has the Son has life. The one who doesn't have the Son of God does not have life. I have written these things to you who believe in the name of the Son of God, so that you may know that you have eternal life" (1 John 5:11-13).

Read that last paragraph again.

It's so simple. If you have Jesus, you have eternal life. It's a promise from God. And, yes, you can *know* that you have eternal life in this present life, simply by believing "in the name of the Son of God."

No guessing game.

No hoping if you're good enough.

It's not about you or me, it's about Jesus. Because He is righteous, I am made righteous by faith in Him.

There is no greater Gift.

Have you received this free Gift of eternal life, with no more pain, grief, or death in Heaven?

Have you shared this great news with someone lately?

"When this corruptible is clothed
with incorruptibility,
and this mortal is clothed
with immortality,
then the saying that is written will take place:
Death has been swallowed up in victory.
Death, where is your victory?
Death, where is your sting?
Now the sting of death is sin,
and the power of sin is the law.
But thanks be to God, who gives us the victory
through our Lord Jesus Christ!"

Paul the Apostle
1 Corinthians 15:54-57

Heaven is...

14

Forever Young

"When I was a boy of 14, my father was so ignorant I could hardly stand to have the old man around. But when I got to be 21, I was astonished at how much the old man had learned in seven years" (attributed to Mark Twain).

Did you have that same realization toward your father (or mother) as you passed through teenage-dom? I did. Thankfully, we don't remain teenagers here on Earth, but rather progress toward maturity.

When you were young, did you wish you were older so that you could get a driver's license, or go on a date, or go to college, or buy a beer?

Now that you're older, do you wish you were younger, or at least looked younger? Many people do. Why?

Maybe because that's when we were in our prime physically, or when we were most attractive, or when life was simpler.

How much time and money are spent each year by people wanting to look and feel younger? It's astronomical. Face creams, lotions, make-up, Botox injections, face-lifts, hair coloring, wrinkle treatments, clothing styles, teeth-whitening, exercise programs and equipment, gym membership, etc.

Is it wrong to want to look and feel younger? No.

Can that desire be taken to an extreme at the risk of becoming so self-absorbed that we spend too much money or affect our relationships? Yes.

I believe we all have this inner desire to be forever young from our Creator, and that we *will* be forever young (and healthy) in Heaven.

Jonathan Edwards (1703 – 1758), the American revivalist preacher, philosopher, and theologian, wrote, "The heavenly inhabitants... remain in eternal youth."

"Eternal youth." I'm good with that! And eternal health also awaits us in Heaven.

Marv Besteman, a retired bank president had an NDE after cancer surgery at the University of Michigan Medical Center. It was after visiting hours; he was in great pain and needed rest. Then he was whisked away by two men (angels?) and taken on a short trip through the blue skies. But though he was an elderly man, he felt like a teenager, with no more pain.[1]

Mr. Besteman "felt like a teenager" during his NDE. But was he a teenager? Could he have been in his twenties or thirties while in Heaven? Or even "ageless"?

Hank Hanegraaff, American Christian author and radio host takes a scientific approach when he suggests, "Our DNA is programmed in such a way that, at a particular point, we reach optimal development from a functional perspective. For the most part, it appears that we reach this stage somewhere in our twenties and thirties...If the blueprints for our glorified bodies are in the DNA, then it would stand to reason that our bodies will be resurrected at the optimal stage of development determined by our DNA."[2]

In *The Great Divorce*, C. S. Lewis portrays Heaven's population as being without age. "No one in that company struck me as being of any particular age. One gets glimpses, even in our country, of that which is ageless - heavy thought in the face of an infant, and frolic childhood in that of a very old man."[3]

The youthfulness can exist in any person, no matter their age at death. Since Heaven also promises no more pain or sickness, we will *never* feel old.

Who wouldn't want that?

This eternal youthfulness has been studied by Bible scholars and teachers, and some make a good case that dwellers of Heaven, in their new bodies, will appear to be in their 30's. This includes people who died before reaching that age.[4]

Thomas Aquinas (1225-1274) the influential Italian priest and theologian, believed that people in Heaven will likely be the age of Jesus Christ when He was crucified, died, and resurrected...about thirty-three years young. Aquinas wrote, "...human nature will be brought back by the resurrection of the state of its ultimate perfection, which is in the state of youth, toward which the movement of growth is terminated, and from which the movement of degeneration begins."[5]

Yes, there IS a real "fountain of youth"...it's found in Heaven. Any family members or friends of ours who had faith in Christ when they died are already enjoying it. I plan to join them. How about you?

Do you want eternal youth?

Do you know someone else who does?

"Therefore we do not give up.
Even though our outer person is being destroyed,
our inner person is being renewed day by day.
For our momentary light affliction is producing for
us an absolutely incomparable
eternal weight of glory.
So we do not focus on what is seen,
but on what is unseen.
For what is seen is temporary,
but what is unseen is eternal."

Paul the Apostle
2 Corinthians 4:16-18

Heaven is...

15

You at Your Best

Do you wonder sometimes why you exist?

Have you ever wished you were someone else?

Do you sometimes get frustrated at your own
weaknesses and failures?

Have you ever felt insignificant, or been told you
were worthless?

I think we've all had these questions or
situations at one time or another.

But rest assured: there is only one you – in the
whole universe. That makes you pretty special from the
very start. Your fingerprint, your iris, your face, and
your personality make you as unique as the individual
snowflake, or each star in the night sky. No two are the
same. Even identical twins have differences.

Your individuality develops as you grow older.
You become more aware of your strengths, talents, and
limitations. Some of us discover early on how to use
them, others learn later in life. And some,
unfortunately, never figure it out.

Here on Earth, we can get a glimpse of who we really are when we put our trust in our Maker. Then He, through His Holy Spirit, can help us be the person He created us to be, with our own unique personality and creativity.

The auto manufacturer includes an owner's manual for your car, in order to get the most potential from your car's performance.

The same goes with our "Manufacturer." He provided an owner's manual for our lives, in order to reach our highest potential; to become the best "me."

From our owner's manual (the Bible):

"Your word is a lamp for my feet and a light on my path" (Psalm 119:105).

"All Scripture is inspired by God and is profitable for teaching, for rebuking, for correcting, for training in righteousness, so that the man of God may be complete, equipped for every good work" (2 Timothy 3:16-17).

So, while we're on Earth, we can learn to improve ourselves. But when a believer in Jesus dies and goes to Heaven, his/her personality doesn't end. Rather, it takes on its fullest, most complete form. You will be the BEST you...forever!

In C. S. Lewis' space trilogy he describes our current human condition as "bent" forms of what our Creator desired. This is the result of our free will, which He also gave us. So, all my selfishness, apathy, lust, even my impairments and illnesses are not the real me. They are only brief aberrations that will be done away with in Heaven and on the New Earth. Then, and only then, will we be the person God created us to be.

You are not the result of a cosmic chance. You were designed.

When you look at a computer and wonder how it came together, you conclude it came from a manufacturer, after it was designed. It didn't just happen by chance. To think it was by chance, is to think irrationally.

We were also designed. But why? The first question of the Westminster Catechism[1] says it well:

Q. 1. What is the chief end of man?
A. Man's chief end is to glorify God, and to enjoy him forever.

Is God a narcissist for wanting us to "glorify" Him and "enjoy him forever"? Of course not. He only wants us to be at our happiest and most complete, which only happens when we trust Him, and the words in His Owner's Manual.

King David knew how to be the best version of himself. Take a few minutes to read Psalm 86 right now. If that doesn't encourage you, check your pulse.

Did you read it yet?

If you ever feel insignificant or worthless, realize first of all that you're not alone. Many have. But also ponder your intrinsic value, simply because you were made in the image of God:

"So God created man in His own image; He created him in the image of God; He created them male and female" (Genesis 1:27).

Being made in God's image simply means you bear some resemblance to your Maker. He has a sense of sight, hearing, smelling, and touching. So do you. He speaks, you speak. The Bible tells us He has breath, so do you. He has hands, you have hands.

A 100-dollar bill (Federal Reserve Note) has a face value of $100, but an intrinsic value of essentially zero…it's only made of paper. A 1-oz gold American Eagle coin has a face value of $50, but an intrinsic value of more than twenty times its face value (check its latest spot price online). That's because it contains gold, a rare metal.

Likewise, you have intrinsic value because you contain the image of God.

God made you to be *you* only, not anyone else. You are an expression of God's creativity. There's no need to try to be someone you're not. He created you to be *you*, with your personality, strengths, talents… and limitations.

We all have something to share with the world. The question is: Will I be a part of the problems in the world, or a part of the solution? I believe it was Eleanor

Roosevelt who said (quoting a Chinese proverb), "Don't curse the darkness, light a candle."

I sometimes get frustrated with my weaknesses; whether it be forgetfulness, selfish desires, lack of planning ahead, or lack of boldness. But that's part of being human on this Earth. With discipline and reliance on God's strength, we can improve our lives, just as a car's performance improves with proper attention and maintenance.

Apostle Paul wrote, "I am able to do all things through Him who strengthens me" (Philippians 4:13).

I'm comforted in knowing that even though I'm not perfect, God still loves me and wants the best for me.

"For He knows what we are made of, remembering that we are dust" (Psalm 103:14).

Even though we have weaknesses, we have great potential, too. Do you realize who you really are? Do others know the real you? God knows you better than anyone, and still loves you.

Another one of my all-time favorite authors is J. R. R. Tolkien. In *The Lord of the Rings*, one key character's true identity is unknown to most. But as his new friends get to know him, his full identity is slowly revealed. Mark Buchanan, in his book *Things Unseen*, writes about the drifter named Strider:

"To everyone else, you look like... well, yourself... But God knows who you really are."

"In J. R. R. Tolkien's *The Lord of the Rings*, four hobbits set out from their beloved and serene home in the Shire on a perilous journey. Early on, they stop at a pub at the edge of the Shire. They meet there a hard-bitten, wind-scoured man named Strider. The locals think Strider's a vagabond, a lone and eccentric drifter. But the hobbits discover something else about him: He's a Ranger, a warrior who roams the edges of the countryside and keeps the towns safe, unknown to those whose lives his vigilance protects daily."

"But that is only the first surprise about Strider. Bit by bit, as the journey deepens and becomes more dangerous, new aspects of Strider emerge. His name is really Aragorn, and he is a man of remarkable wisdom, skill, boldness. He is respected or feared in the halls of great power. But even these revelations do not prepare his fellow travellers for the most amazing truth of all: Aragorn is the hereditary heir of all Middle-earth. He is the long-awaited One. He is the supreme king, the King of kings."

"Strider? That scruffy, patchy vagrant? The very same. It was just hidden for a time."[2]

"You are a new creation, an heir and coheir with Jesus Christ. The old has gone; the new has come. Only, what you are has not yet been made known. It is true, but for now it is hidden. To those unaware, you might look like anybody, like nobody. You might appear merely a taxicab driver, a homemaker, a lawyer, a 7-Eleven clerk, a vagabond, even. But the divine truth is that the old you has died, and the new you is waiting for the right moment to be revealed."[3]

That moment, for the believer in Jesus, is the one immediately after your last breath here on Earth, when you enter Heaven. You'll be the "you" you have always longed for.

At age thirty-three, a woman named Crystal was hospitalized with pancreatitis. Due to some complications, she clinically died. She found herself in Heaven with a new awareness and certainty of who she really was. All her earthly weaknesses were stripped away and she saw herself as she truly was – the whole person that God had created.[4]

In Jeremiah 1:5 God says, "Before I formed you in the womb, I knew you."

In Heaven, we will finally meet ourselves...and it will be the *best* version.

Do you want to be the best you... forever?

Have you entrusted your life to your Maker?

"For now we see only a reflection as in a mirror;
then we shall see face to face.
Now I know in part; then I shall know fully, even as
I am fully known."

Paul the Apostle
1 Corinthians 13:12

16

A Mansion and Wealth

A mansion is "a large and impressive house: the large house of a wealthy person" (Merriam-Webster Dictionary).

Have you ever visited a mansion?

I can remember visiting The Breakers in Newport, Rhode Island, and the Biltmore in Asheville, North Carolina, and Versailles, just outside of Paris, France. The beauty and vastness of these "homes" is utterly stunning, leaving you breathless.

But they are just a small hint of what Jesus has in store for His followers. In John 14:12, He promised, "In my Father's house are many mansions: if *it were* not *so,* I would have told you. I go to prepare a place for you."

Do you realize that Jesus Christ is preparing a place for you in Heaven? Ancient Jewish culture provided that a bridegroom would build on a room to his father's house to accommodate the new couple.

American theologian Jonathan Edwards wrote, "To go to heaven, fully to enjoy God, is *infinitely better than the most pleasant accommodations here.* Better than fathers and mothers, husbands, wives or children, or the company of any, or all earthly friends. These are but shadows; but the enjoyment of God is the substance. These are but scattered beams; but God is the sun. These are but streams; but God is the fountain. These are but drops; but God is the ocean"[1] (emphasis mine).

Captain Dale Black, during his NDE after his small plane crashed into a stone edifice at 135 mph, plunging 70 feet to the ground, was stunned by what he saw soon after his spirit left his body. He quickly drew near to a glorious and brilliant, light-filled city, surrounded by smaller towns and villages. The homes were colorful and custom-made, yet they all fit together well like pieces in a puzzle. He felt like he was made for this place, and did not want to return to Earth.[2]

The apostle John, one of Jesus' closest of the Twelve Disciples, had been exiled to the Greek island of Patmos, off the west coast of present-day Turkey. The Roman Emperor Domitian was known for his persecution of Christians. While in exile there, John did not have a near-death experience. However, you might say he had a "near-Life experience."

He saw the Creator of Life, and a glorious vision of the future abode of His bride, the church - those who believe and trust in Him. I'll let John tell you in his own words:

"I, John, your brother and partner in the tribulation, kingdom, and endurance that are in Jesus, was on the island called Patmos because of God's Word and the testimony about Jesus. I was in the Spirit on the Lord's Day, and I heard a loud voice behind me like a trumpet saying, 'Write on a scroll what you see and send it to the seven churches: Ephesus, Smyrna, Pergamum, Thyatira, Sardis, Philadelphia, and Laodicea.'"

"I turned to see whose voice it was that spoke to me. When I turned I saw seven gold lampstands, and among the lampstands was One like the Son of Man, dressed in a long robe and with a gold sash wrapped around His chest.

"His head and hair were white like wool — white as snow — and His eyes like a fiery flame. His feet were like fine bronze as it is fired in a furnace, and His voice like the sound of cascading waters. He had seven stars in His right hand; a sharp double-edged sword came from His mouth, and His face was shining like the sun at midday."

"When I saw Him, I fell at His feet like a dead man. He laid His right hand on me and said, 'Don't be afraid! I am the First and the Last, and the Living One. I was dead, but look — I am alive forever and ever, and I hold the keys of death and Hades. Therefore write what you have seen, what is, and what will take place after this'" (Revelation 2:9-19).

"Then I saw a new heaven and a new earth, for the first heaven and the first earth had passed away, and the sea no longer existed. I also saw the holy city, the new Jerusalem, coming down out of heaven from God, prepared like a bride adorned for her husband. Then I heard a loud voice from the throne: 'Look! God's dwelling is with humanity, and He will live with them. They will be His people, and God Himself will be with them and be their God. He will wipe away every tear from their eyes. Death will no longer exist; grief, crying, and pain will exist no longer, because the previous things have passed away.'

Then the One seated on the throne said, 'Look! I am making everything new.'
He also said, 'Write, because these words are faithful and true'" (Revelation 21:1-5).

How could anyone not have this desire for a glorious dwelling to live in forever?

In Mathew Henry's Concise Commentary, we read, "The happiness of heaven is spoken of as in a father's house. There are many mansions, for there are many sons to be brought to glory. Mansions are lasting dwellings. Christ will be the Finisher of that of which he is the Author or Beginner; if he has prepared the place for us, he will prepare us for it."

As Christians, we are being prepared for a heavenly mansion!

Let that sink in.

No matter what kind of dwelling we live in here on Earth, believers have a mansion in the sky, built by the Creator of the universe, who loves us!

The lyrics to the gospel song "Mansion Over the Hilltop," written by Ira Stanphill and sung by Elvis Presley and many others, say it well. Look them up if you're not familiar with the song.

Jesus often spoke of the treasure awaiting those who follow His truth:

In Matthew 6:20 Jesus said, "But collect for yourselves treasures in heaven, where neither moth nor rust destroys, and where thieves don't break in and steal."

"The kingdom of heaven is like treasure, buried in a field that a man found and reburied. Then in his joy he goes and sells everything he has and buys that field" (Matthew 13:44).

"Then, looking at him, Jesus loved him and said to him, 'You lack one thing: Go, sell all you have and give to the poor, and you will have treasure in heaven. Then come, follow Me'" (Mark 10:21).

The apostle Paul also wrote about the inheritance and riches awaiting followers of Christ:

"And my God will meet all your needs according to the riches of His glory in Christ Jesus" (Philippians 4:19).

"I pray that the perception of your mind may be enlightened so you may know what is the hope of His calling, what are the glorious riches of His inheritance among the saints" (Ephesians 1:18).

"For you know the grace of our Lord Jesus Christ: Though He was rich, for your sake He became poor, so that by His poverty you might become rich" (2 Corinthians 8:9).

If you work at a job, your employer may provide some benefits as part of their compensation to you. This might include insurance coverage for medical and dental costs, retirement savings accounts, vacation pay, maternity leave, etc. There is a long list of benefits for the believer in Jesus. Psalm 103:2 says, "...do not forget all His benefits." Read the entire Psalm for the list.

And this inherited wealth is reserved in Heaven for you right now, as a follower of Christ. The apostle Peter wrote:

"Praise the God and Father of our Lord Jesus Christ. According to His great mercy, He has given us a new birth into a living hope through the resurrection of Jesus Christ from the dead and into an inheritance that is imperishable, uncorrupted, and unfading, kept in heaven for you" (1 Pet 1:3-4).

Do you realize that God the Father earnestly longs to share His kingdom with you and me? Jesus said:

"But seek His kingdom, and these things will be provided for you. Don't be afraid, little flock, because your Father delights to give you the kingdom" (Luke 12:31-32).

Have you reserved your spot in the heavenly mansion prepared for you?

Are you, by faith and obedience, laying up treasures in Heaven?

"In my Father's house are many mansions:
if *it were* not *so*, I would have told you.
I go to prepare a place for you."

Jesus Christ
(John 14:2, KJV)

Heaven is...

17

New Adventures Forever

In the beginning of J. R. R. Tolkien's epic, high-fantasy novel, *The Hobbit*, Gandalf – the wise and bearded wizard - coyly tells Bilbo – the simple agrarian hobbit – of the difficulty he's having in finding someone to go on an adventure with him. Bilbo explains that hobbits are home-bodies and have absolutely no desire to leave their comfortable surroundings of their hometown, Hobbiton.

But after some deliberation, Bilbo has a change of attitude, and subsequently begins the adventure of his life, which he never regrets.

Bilbo and his friends learn just what he is made of.[1]

What adventures have you gone on?

When you were a child, did your family travel to the mountains, the beach, the lake, a national park, another city, or another country? Maybe it was a well-deserved vacation, or an unexpected excursion to a place you've never been before.

Are you one who enjoys extreme adventures that test your physical stamina and courage?

Do you remember the feeling you had when you saw new places and new sights for the first time? Or when you learned new things?

The U. S. Navy used to have as its slogan, "It's not just a job, it's an adventure!" I found that to be very true. From boot camp in San Diego, California, to submarine school in Groton, Connecticut, to my first submarine assignment (and three more after that), my life consisted of learning the submarines' systems and capabilities, being tested on my knowledge, and finally earning my "dolphins."

Then there were the top-secret Cold War missions, Desert Storm, and cruises to new lands through vast oceans. From Groton, to Norfolk, to Bermuda, to the Virgin Islands, Cape Canaveral, Fort Lauderdale, to Scotland, Italy, Corfu (Greece), France, Gibraltar, Hawaii, Hong Kong, Curacao (Netherlands Antilles), Panama Canal, Okinawa, South Korea, and Japan. On occasion, while my boat was in an upkeep period in Scotland or Italy, a few shipmates and I would travel by train, bus, or ferry to more new adventures in Switzerland, Germany, England, or Holland.

My Navy travels allowed me to enjoy amazing sights and sounds like Shakespeare's Globe Theatre in London, the British Museum, The Louvre, Notre Dame and the Eiffel Tower in Paris, Versailles Palace, the Vatican and Sistine Chapel, the catacombs and Coliseum in Rome, Pompei and Mount Vesuvius, the Leaning Tower of Pisa, DaVinci's original Last Supper painting in Milan, the Rembrandt Museum in Amsterdam, Ground Zero in Nagasaki, Mount Pilatus and The Matterhorn in Switzerland (had to buy a Swiss Army knife in Zermatt!).

I loved it! Like many people, I'm hungry for more new adventures, and even a repeat of some of the past ones!

And I haven't even mentioned all the USA destinations I've experienced.

Did you ever want to take a rocket to space? As a young boy growing up during the 1960's "space race," I was enthralled with the rockets launched into Earth orbit, and on to orbit the moon, and then Apollo 11's first landing on our moon 238,900 miles away. Yep... I watched it on our black and white TV with my parents. As a kid I wanted to be an astronaut. I built the model kit of the lunar module.

Today, I imagine what it would be like to ride in a space shuttle, to visit the moon, or Mars.

There are other worlds. Our universe is infinite in scope. When you look up into the sky, you're looking at infinity.

The infinite God has not only created a present Heaven and present Earth, but also an infinite New Heaven and New Earth promised to His family of believers, those who have accepted His free gift of forgiveness and eternal life in Jesus (re-read Revelations 21).

So, if you love adventure, you'll really love Heaven!

I believe that our longing for excitement and adventure is yet another desire that our Creator gave us, and not for this life only, but for the next - in eternity. Can you imagine what heavenly adventures might be like? Whatever they are, you can bet they'll make our earthly experiences seem pale and even boring in comparison. Do you think that our Creator would put this thirst for adventure within us, and then remove it when we die? I don't. And even though some people currently live with physical challenges or emotional aversion to thrills, these are earthly, transitory states. In Heaven and on the New Earth that is coming, you will be a *new you*, equipped to explore, to learn, to absorb all that God has prepared for those who love Him.

In the first century A.D., the apostle Paul wrote (quoting the prophet Isaiah who lived about 700 years earlier):

> "But as it is written: 'What eye did not see and ear did not hear, and what never entered the human mind—God prepared this for those who love Him'" (1 Corinthians 2:9).

It's impossible to imagine all the adventures and wonders that await us in Heaven. But we can rest assured that it will be infinitely better than any adventure we can have in our physical lifetime.

Just ask Eben Alexander, a Harvard-trained neurosurgeon, who wrote about his NDE:

"Then I heard a new sound: a living sound, like the richest, most complex, most beautiful piece of music you've ever heard… I began to move up. Fast. There was a whooshing sound, and in a flash I went through the opening and found myself in a completely new world. The strangest, most beautiful world I'd ever seen. Brilliant, vibrant, ecstatic, stunning… I could heap on one adjective after another to describe what this world looked and felt like, but they'd all fall short. I felt like I was being born... Below me there was countryside. It was green, lush, and earthlike. It was earth... but at the same time it wasn't... A beautiful, incredible dream world... Except it wasn't a dream... I was absolutely sure of one thing: this place I'd suddenly found myself in was completely real... Remember who's talking to you right now. I'm not a soft-headed sentimentalist. I know what death looks like... I know my biology, and while I'm not a physicist, I'm no slouch at that, either. I know the difference between fantasy and reality, and I know that the experience I'm struggling to give you the vaguest, most completely unsatisfactory picture of, was the single most real experience of my life."[2]

Are you up for an eternal adventure beyond your wildest dreams?

Are there friends or family members you'd like to take with you?

Infinite adventures in Heaven
await you and me...
if we're followers of Jesus.

18

Home

"Welcome Home!"

Two of the most comforting words to hear, especially to the military veteran, the weary traveler, or the prisoner set free.

Many songs have described an inner longing for "home." Can you think of one or two right now?

In "The Wizard of Oz" Dorothy longed for being somewhere over the rainbow. Haven't you? Then afterwards, she longed for being home again: "There's no place like home! There's no place like home!" she said.

Isn't it strange that we possess both longings at the same time? To be somewhere else AND to be home? I believe God put those desires in us, and they'll both be fully satisfied in Heaven.

Pastor Mark Buchanan's book *"Things Unseen"* talks about these two longings:
"Why won't we be bored in heaven?
Because it's the one place where both
impulses – to go beyond and to go home
– are perfectly joined and totally
satisfied.

It's the one place where we're constantly
discovering – where everything is always
fresh and the possessing of a thing is as
 good as the pursuing of it – and yet
where we are fully at home
– where everything is as it ought to be
and where we find, undiminished, that
mysterious something we never found
down here...And this lifelong
melancholy that hangs on us, this
wishing we were someone else
somewhere else, vanishes too. Our
craving to go beyond is always and fully
realized. Our yearning for home is once
and for all fulfilled. The *ahh!* of deep
satisfaction and the *aha!* of delighted
surprise meet, and they kiss."[1]

Do you ever feel like a pilgrim on this earth, just
passing through until you reach your real home?

I sure do. I've discovered that my Creator put
that longing within me. The wise King Solomon
expressed it this way:

"He [God] has made everything appropriate in
its time. He has also put eternity in their hearts, but
man cannot discover the work God has done from
beginning to end" (Ecclesiastes 3:11).

We each have "eternity" in our heart... an
eternal, spiritual part of us that longs for eternal
things... like the things I've shared in this book.

Colin Duriez, in his book *Tolkien and C.S. Lewis –
The Gift of Friendship*, comments on Lewis' longing for
"home":

"Lewis saw this unquenchable longing as a sure sign that no part of the created world, and thus no aspect of our experience, is capable of fulfilling humankind. We are dominated by a [feeling of] homelessness, and yet by a keen sense of what 'home' means."[2]

What does "home" mean to you?

For most people, it evokes thoughts of being where you are loved, and where you can rest comfortably and find solace. For others who aren't as fortunate, home can be a lonely or dangerous place.

God has invited us into His Home in Heaven... a Home that will mean everlasting love and joy and rest. All we have to do is accept the invitation.

King David had his eyes fixed on his eternal home when he wrote the Shepherd's Psalm:

"Only goodness and faithful love will pursue me all the days of my life, and I will dwell in the house of the LORD as long as I live" (Psalm 23:6).

While I was writing this book, the Rev. Billy Graham went Home to Heaven at the age of 99. He is known for saying:

"Someday you will read or hear that Billy Graham is dead. Don't you believe a word of it! I shall be more alive than I am now. I will just have changed my address. I will have gone into the presence of God."[3]

Billy Graham was influenced by another great evangelist, Dwight L. Moody. In his autobiography he wrote:

"Someday you will read in the papers that D. L. Moody, of East Northfield, is dead. Don't you believe a word of it! At that moment I shall be more alive than I am now.

"I shall have gone up higher, that is all; out of this old clay tenement into a house that is immortal — a body that death cannot touch; that sin cannot taint; a body fashioned like unto His glorious body."[4]

A lady whose name is Crystal had an NDE. She found her temporary visit to heaven very difficult to describe:

"The hardest thing for me is finding the words to fully describe what I experienced in heaven, because there are no human words that even come close. I grasp at words like 'beautiful' and 'brilliant' and 'amazing,' but they are wildly inadequate. What I experienced in heaven was so real and so lucid and so utterly intense, it made my experiences on Earth seem hazy and out of focus - as if heaven is the reality and life as we know it is just a dream... It was a feeling of absolute purity and perfection, of something completely unblemished and unbroken, and being immersed in it filled me with the kind of peace and assurance I'd never known on Earth. It was like being bathed in love. It was a brightness I didn't just see, but felt. And it felt familiar, like something I remembered, or even recognized. The best way to put it is this: I was home."[5]

Heaven is home. Forever.

Don't be left out. Trust Jesus to take you there.

Do you want to go Home forever when your life on Earth ends?

Is there someone you'd like to have join you there?

"...and we are confident and satisfied
to be out of the body
and at home
with the Lord."

Paul the Apostle
(2 Corinthians 5:8)

Heaven is...

Heaven is...

If you found this book helpful, please tell your friends, and consider writing a brief review on Amazon.

If you're on Facebook, I also invite you to Like the book's Facebook page (search the book's title), and then scroll to the Recommendations and Reviews section to recommend it.

Thank you

Heaven is...

NOTES

Introduction

1. For more NDE stories from the person who coined the term "near-death experience," consult Dr. Raymond Moody, Jr.'s classic international best-seller, *Life After Life* (originally published in 1975).

2. C. S. Lewis, *Mere Christianity*, (Macmillan Paperbacks Edition, 1960), 120.

Chapter 1 - Like Eternal Sex

1. Mark Twain, *Letters from the Earth*, ed. by Bernard DeVoto, Harper and Row, 1962 (written *ca.* 1909).

2. For example, see: Richard Eby, *Caught Up into Paradise* (Old Tappan, NJ: Revell, 1978).

3. Randy Alcorn, *Heaven*, (Carol Stream, IL: Tyndale House Publishers, 2004), 352.

4. For more on the intimacy aspect and an excellent compilation of stories of people's near-death experiences, see: John Burke, *Imagine Heaven* (Grand Rapids MI: Baker Books, a division of Baker Publishing Group, 2015).

5. Thomas Purifoy, Jr., *Why Sex is the Best Argument For Creation – and Against Evolution,* https://isgenesishistory.com/why-sex-is-the-best-argument-for-creation-against-evolution/?goal=0_052697a034-dd485a64c7-149811913&mc_cid=dd485a64c7&mc_eid=60f24a e57a

6. One example of this teaching, from a Messianic Jewish source, is "Hebrew Wedding Traditions – A Type and Shadow of Jesus and His Church", posted at: https://shoutingthemessage.wordpress.com/2013/11/21/jesus-christ-his-bride-and-the-hebrew-wedding-traditions/ See also "Jewish Wedding Customs and the Bride of Messiah" at: http://messianicfellowship.50webs.com/wedding.html

7. See: Faisal Malick, *10 Amazing Muslims Touched by God,* (Shippensburg, PA: Destiny Image, 2012).

8. Pim Van Lommel, *Consciousness Beyond Life: The Science of the Near-Death Experience* (New York: HarperCollins, 2010), Kindle edition, 34.

9. C. S. Lewis, *The Complete C. S. Lewis Signature Classics: Miracles* (HarperOne, *an imprint of* Harper Collins *Publishers,* 2002), 297-298.

Chapter 2 - True Love and Friendship

1. Charles M. Schulz, *The Complete Peanuts 1959-1960* (Seattle: Fantagraphics Books, Vol 5 © Peanuts International, LLC, 2006), 136.

2. Jenny Sharkey, *Clinically Dead: I've Seen Heaven and Hell* (n.p.: Gospel Media, 2013), Kindle edition, 16.

3. See: Don Piper and Cecil Murphey, *90 Minutes in Heaven: A True Story of Death & Life* (Grand Rapids: Revell, a division of Baker Publishing Group, 2006).

4. See: Sid Roth and Lonnie Lane, *Heaven Is Beyond Your Wildest Expectations: Ten True Stories of Experiencing Heaven* (Shippensburg, PA: Destiny Image, 2012).

Chapter 3 - Real Joy

1. See: Dale Black and Ken Gire, *Flight to Heaven: A Plane Crash...A Lone Survivor...A Journey to Heaven - and Back* (Minneapolis: Bethany House, a division of Baker Publishing Group, 2010).

2. C. S. Lewis, *Letters to Malcolm: Chiefly on Prayer* (Harcourt, Brace, and World, 1963-64), chapter 17, p. 88-93.

Chapter 4 - Universal Peace and Rest

1. Jeffrey Long and Paul Perry, *Evidence of the Afterlife: The Science of Near-Death Experiences*

(New York: HarperCollins, 2009), Kindle edition, 26.

Chapter 5 – Our Ultimate Hope

1. Mark Buchanan, *Things Unseen - Living in Light of Forever*, (Multnomah Publishers, Inc., 2002), 24.
2. See this entry in "The Christ Quake" at https://discussions.godandscience.org/viewtopic.php?t=38866
   Also, Dr. David Reagan gives an informative video tour of the Mt of Olives and mentions the prophecy of an earthquake splitting the Mt of Olives. See https://www.youtube.com/watch?time_continue=221&v=cCNO8AfYyVI

Chapter 6 - Forgiveness

1. Charles H. Spurgeon, *Spurgeon's Morning and Evening Devotions from the Bible*, (Grand Rapids, Michigan: Baker Book House, 1964), 8.
2. Sharkey, *Clinically Dead: I've Seen Heaven and Hell*, Kindle edition, 16.

Chapter 7 - Freedom

1. Albert M. Wolters, *Creation Regained: Biblical Basics for a Reformational Worldview* (Grand Rapids: Eerdmans, 1985), 58.

Chapter 8 - Paradise Beyond Nature

1. C. S. Lewis, "The Weight of Glory" in *The Weight of Glory and Other Addresses*, Harper Collins, 1976, 43-4.

2. For another eyewitness account of paradise, see: Marvin J. Besteman and Lorilee Craker, *My Journey to Heaven: What I Saw and How It Changed My Life*, (Grand Rapids: Baker, a division of Baker Publishing Group, 2012).

3. See: Black and Gire, *Flight to Heaven.*

Chapter 9 - Filled with the Best Music

1. C. S. Lewis, *The Chronicles of Narnia: The Magician's Nephew*, HarperCollins Publishers, 65.

2. See: Black and Gire, *Flight to Heaven.*

3. There are many styles of great music that appeal to diverse tastes. For youthful, positive, and encouraging music on the radio with a message of hope, I highly recommend K-Love (**www.klove.com**), which may have a broadcast radio station near you. Also, Majesty Radio (**www.majestyradio.org**) provides a variety of styles from the '70s to the early 2000s, and "features traditional Christian hymns and instrumental sacred music exalting the power and beauty of God." For selections of choral hymns and orchestral arrangements, visit Hymns Radio (**www.hymnsradio.com**).

Chapter 11 - Having Superpowers

1. Howard Storm, *My Descent into Death: A Second Chance at Life* (New York: Doubleday, 2005), Kindle edition, 26.

2. See: George G. Ritchie and Elizabeth Sherrill, *Return from Tomorrow* (Grand Rapids: Spire, a division of Baker Publishing Group, 1978).

3. Long and Perry, *Evidence of the Afterlife*, 59-60.

Chapter 12 - The Best High

1. www.navigators.org

2. See: Burke, *Imagine Heaven.*

Chapter 13 - No Pain, Grief, or Death

1. Unknown, but often wrongly attributed to Mother Teresa, according to the Mother Teresa Center.

2. See: Bill Wiese, *What Happens When I Die? True Stories of the Afterlife and What They Tell Us about Eternity,* (Lake Mary, FL: Charisma House, 2013).

Chapter 14 - Forever Young

1. See: Besteman and Craker, *My Journey to Heaven.*

2. Taken from *Resurrection* by Hank Hanegraaff, Copyright © 2000, by Hank Hanegraaff. Used by permission of Thomas Nelson. www.thomasnelson.com.

3. C. S. Lewis, *The Great Divorce*, (New York: Macmillan, 1946), 29-30.
4. See: Alister E. McGrath, *A Brief History of Heaven* (Malden, Mass.: Blackwell, 2003).
5. Thomas Aquinas, *Summa Theologica*, supplement, q. 81, art. 1.

Chapter 15 – You at Your Best
1. https://reformed.org/documents/wsc/index.html?mainframe=https://reformed.org/documents/wsc/WSC_frames.html&wsc_text=/documents/wsc/WSC.html, accessed 3/10/19.
2. J. R. R. Tolkien, *The Lord of the Rings*, Book 1 (London: Unwin Paperbacks, 1966), 168-9, as cited in Buchanan, *Things Unseen*, 171.
3. Buchanan, *Things Unseen*, 171-2.
4. See: Burke, *Imagine Heaven*.

Chapter 16 - A Mansion and Wealth
1. Jonathan Edwards, excerpt from a sermon delivered in 1733 entitled "The True Christian's Life, A Journey Towards Heaven" in *The Works of President Edwards*, vol. 4 of 4. (New York: Leavitt & Allen, 1852) 575.
2. See: Black and Gire, *Flight to Heaven*.

Chapter 17 – New Adventures Forever
1. See: J. R. R. Tolkien, *The Hobbit*, (Boston: Houghton Mifflin Company, 1984).

2. Eben Alexander, M.D., *Proof of Heaven* (New York: Simon and Schuster, 2012), Kindle edition, 38-41.

Chapter 18 - Home
1. Buchanan, *Things Unseen*, 77.
2. Colin Duriez, *Tolkien and C.S. Lewis – The Gift of Friendship* (Mahwah, NJ: Hiddenspring, 2003), 56.
3. Caleb Lindgren, "Someday you will read or hear that Billy Graham didn't really say that," *Christianity Today,* (February 21, 2018), http://www.christianitytoday.com/ct/2018/february-web-only/billy-graham-viral-quote-on-death-not-his-d-l-moody.html.
4. Ibid.
5. Crystal McVea and Alex Tresniowski, *Waking Up in Heaven: A True Story of Brokenness, Heaven, and Life Again* (New York: Howard Books, 2013), Kindle edition, locations 239-78.

Heaven is...

Made in the USA
Columbia, SC
06 January 2020